Mandala Coloring Book for Teens

CREATIVE COLORING PRESS

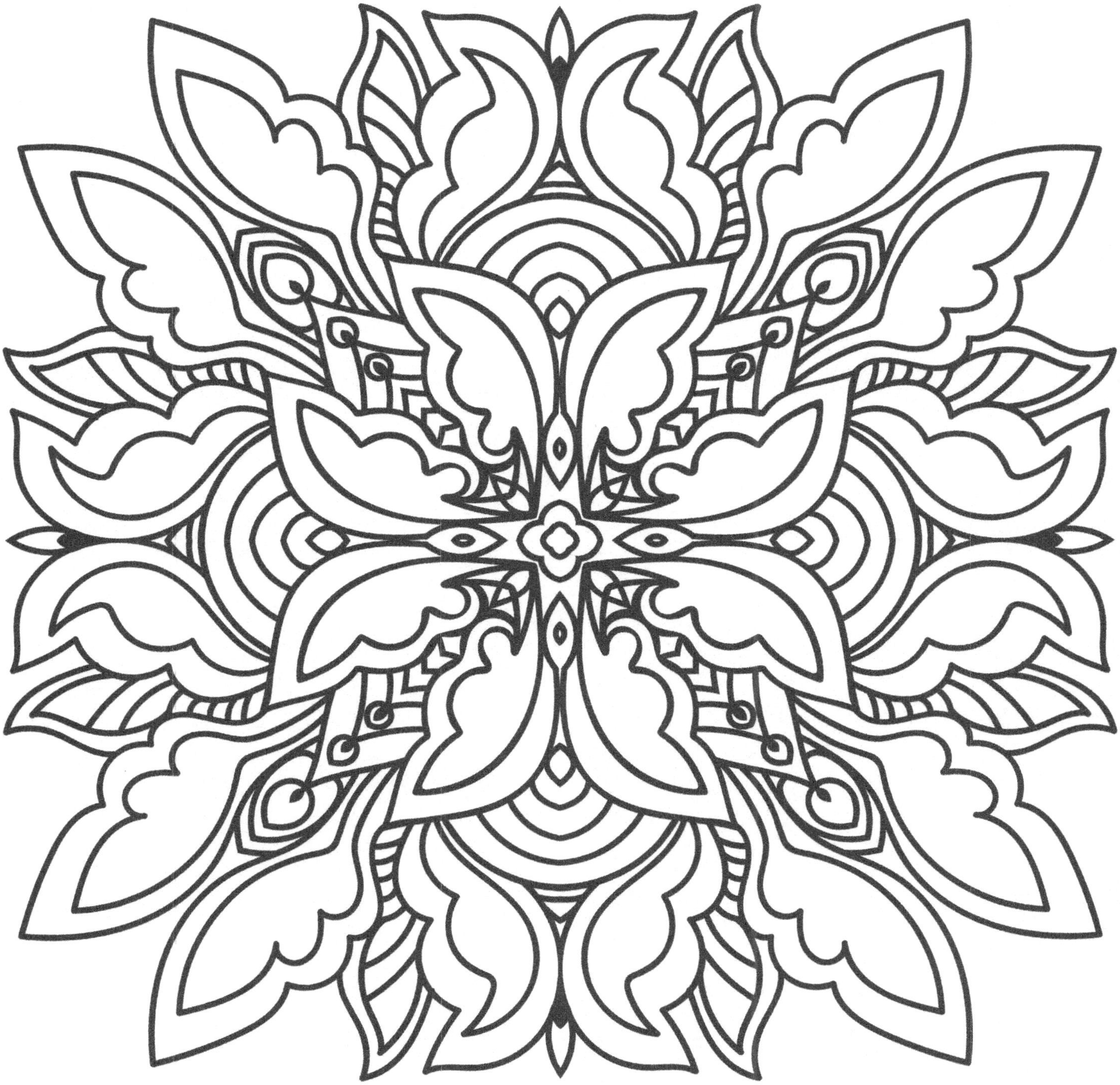

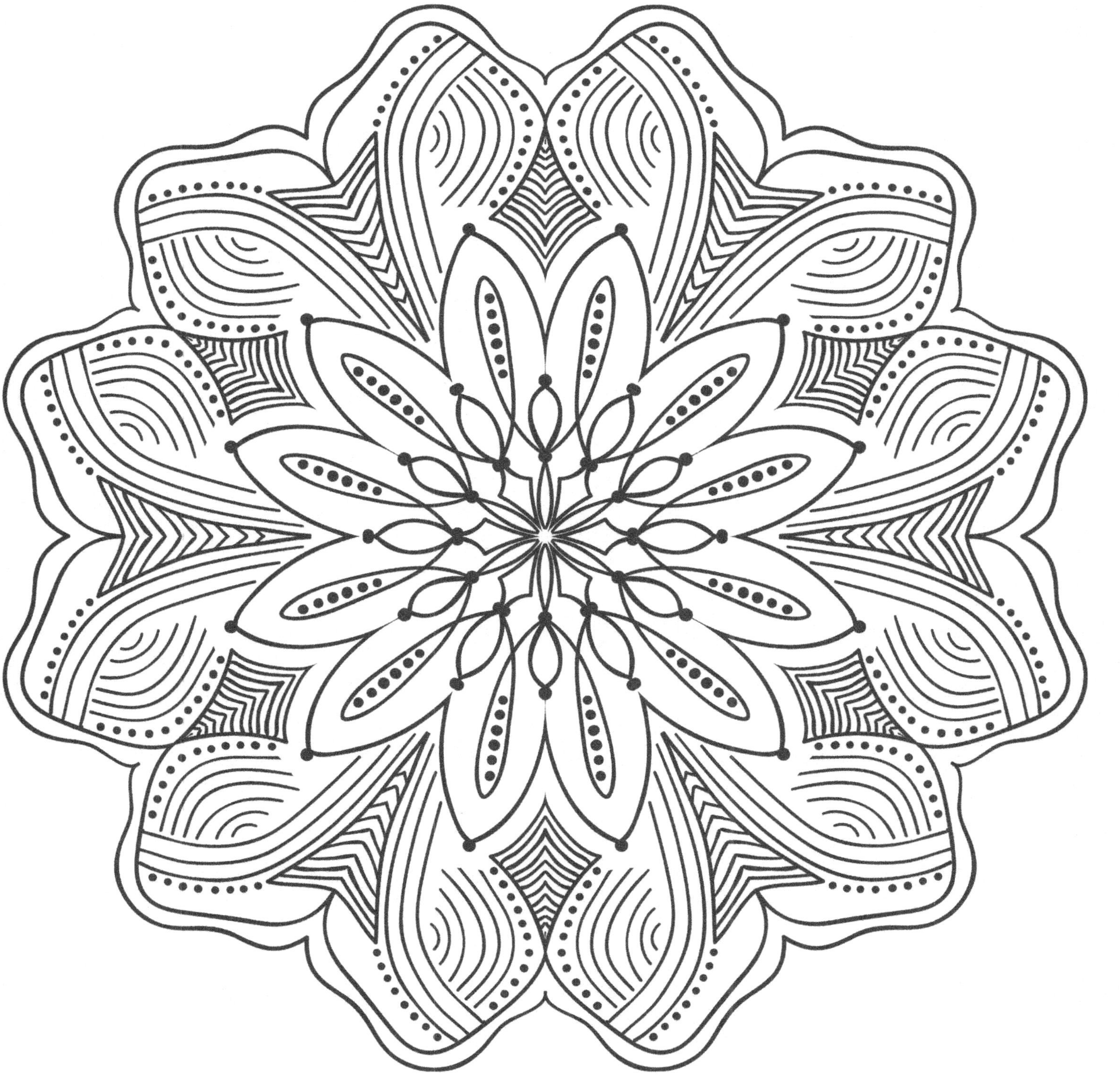

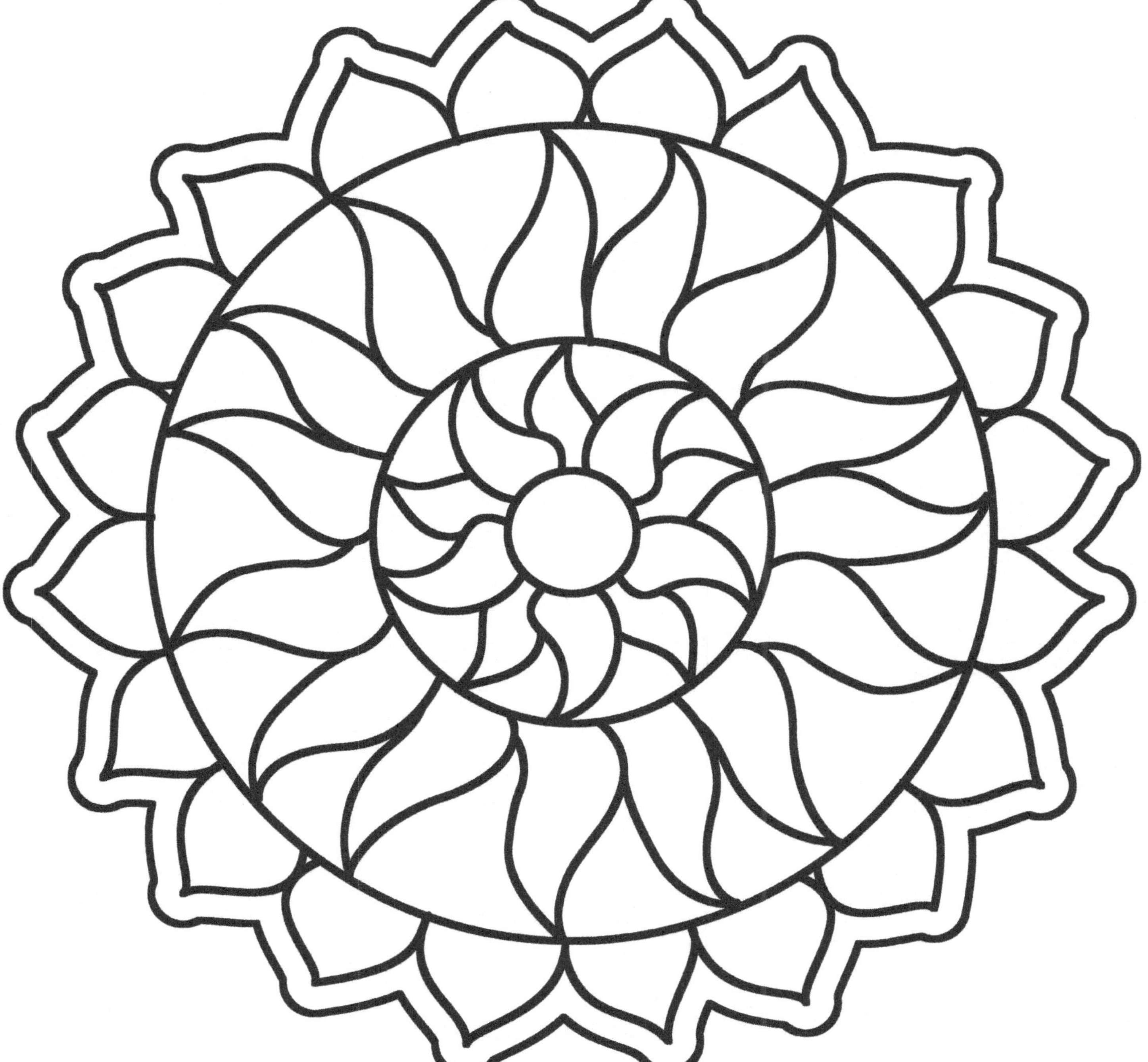

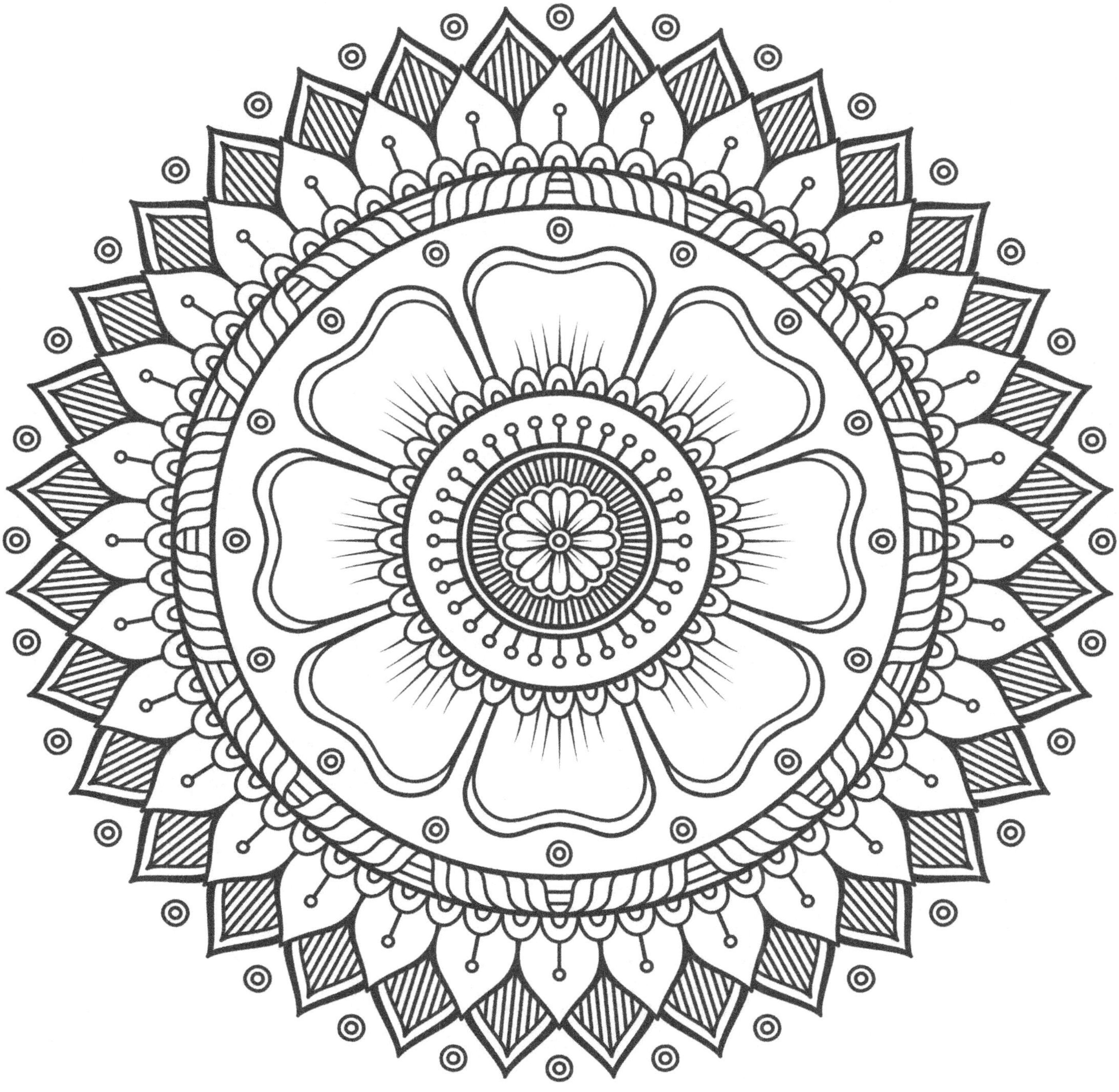

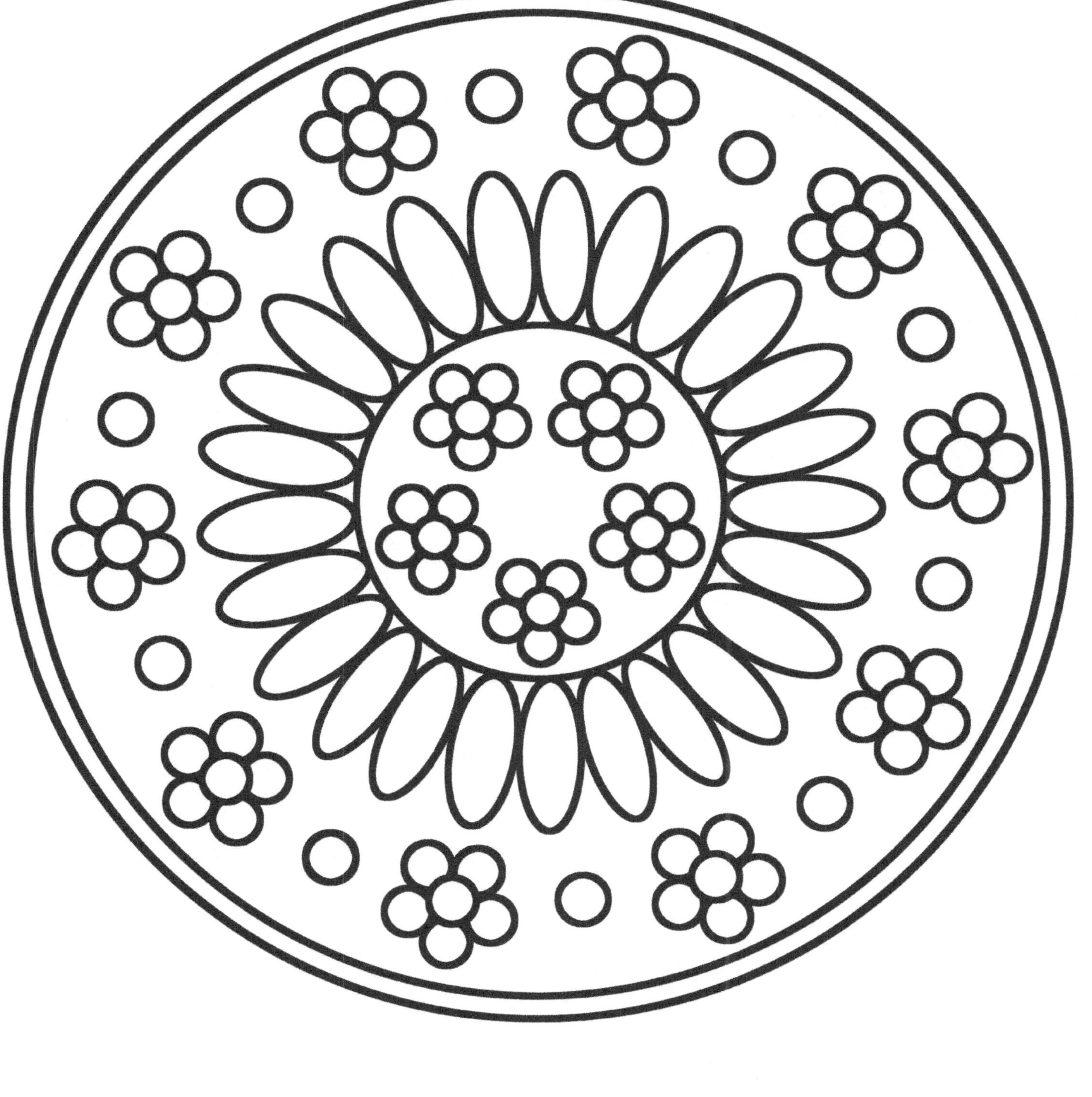

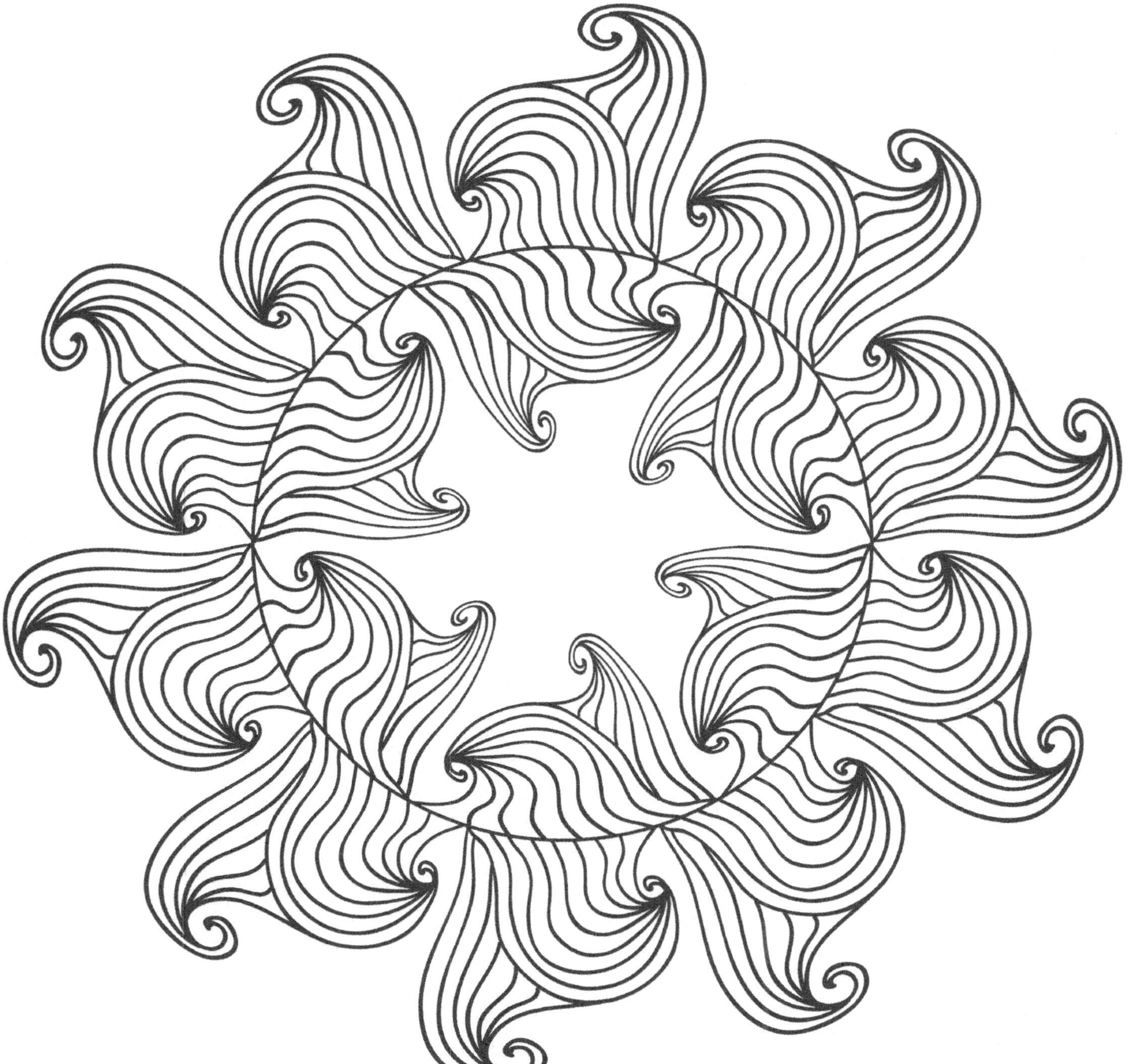

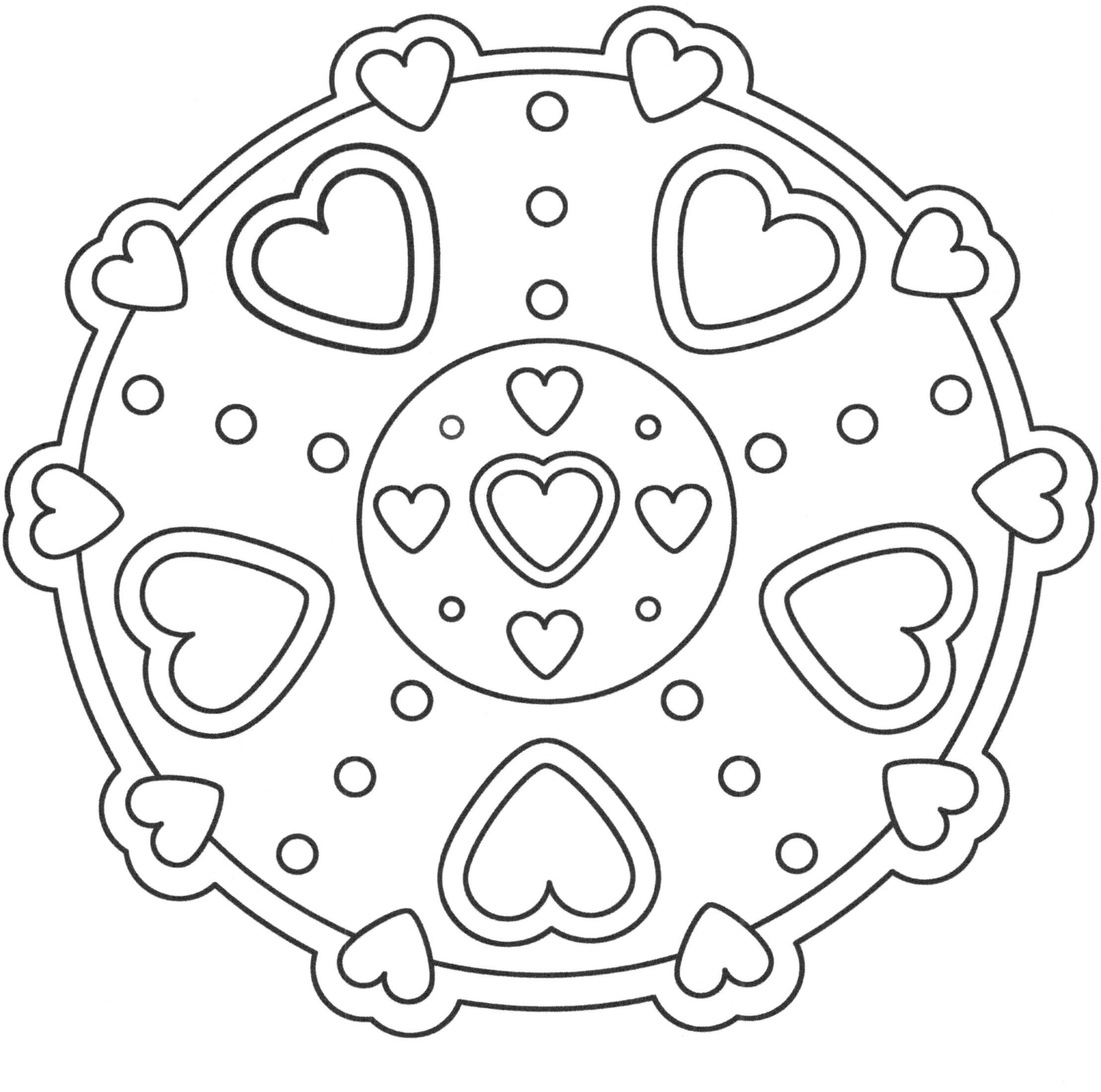

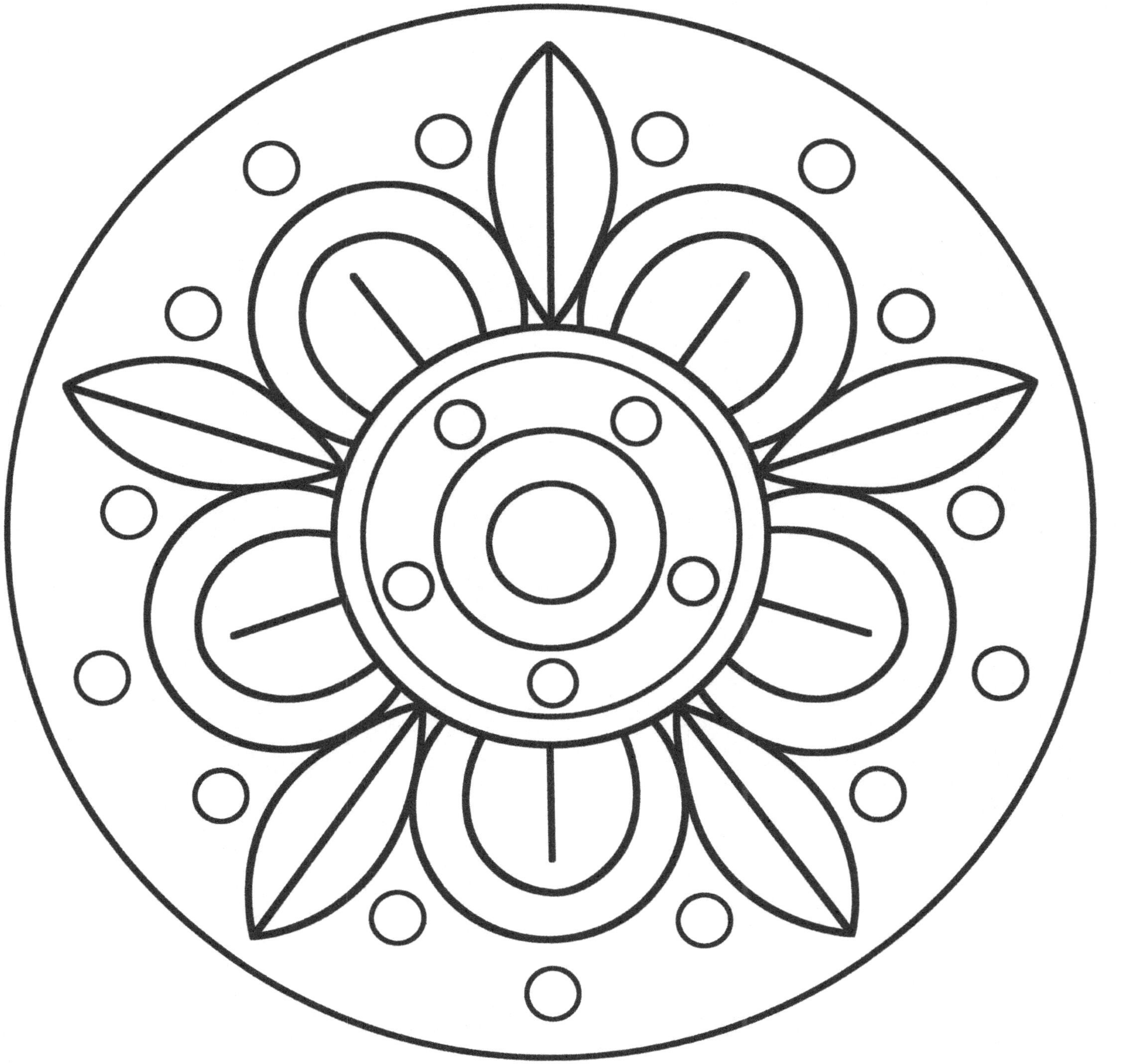

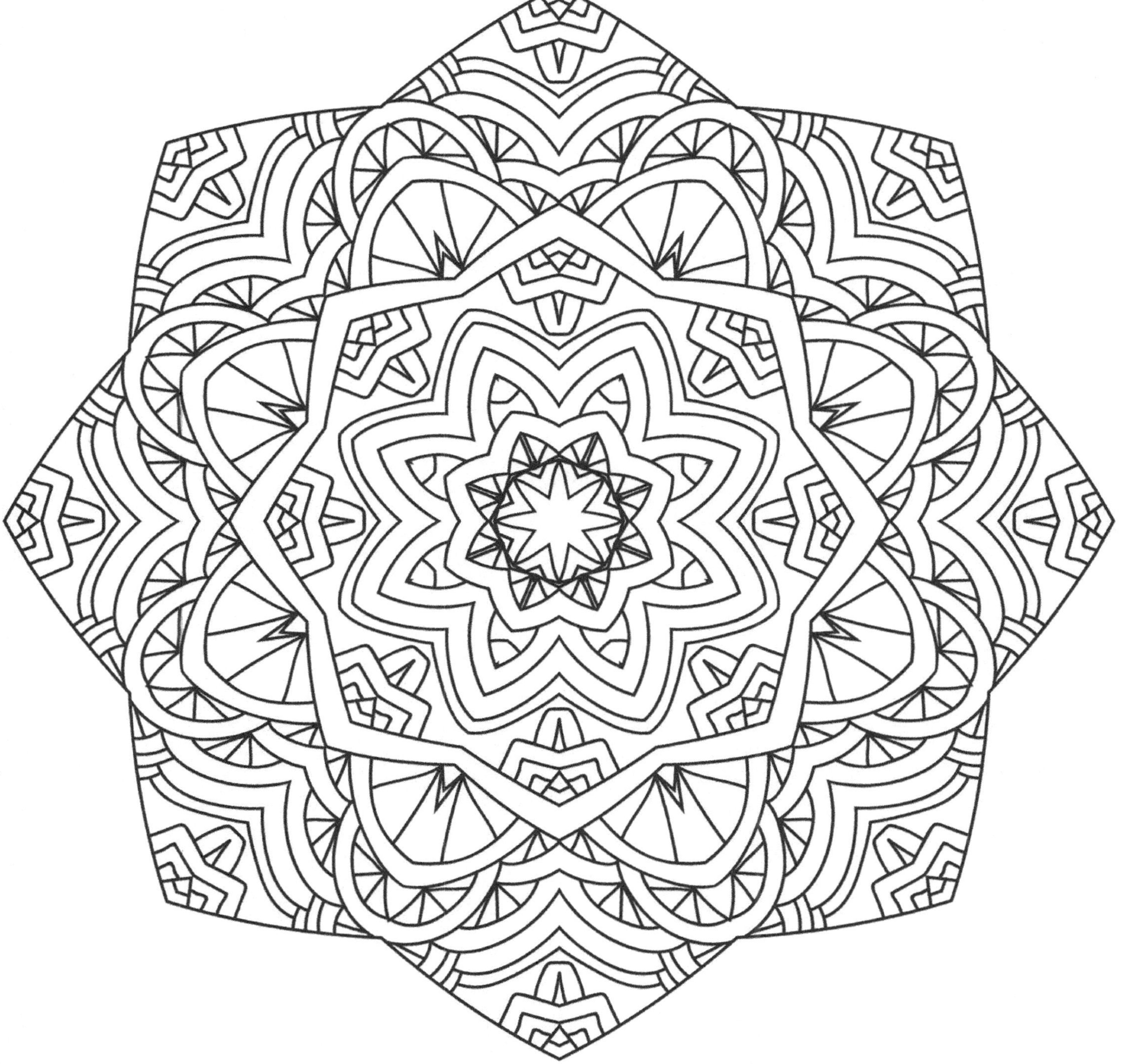

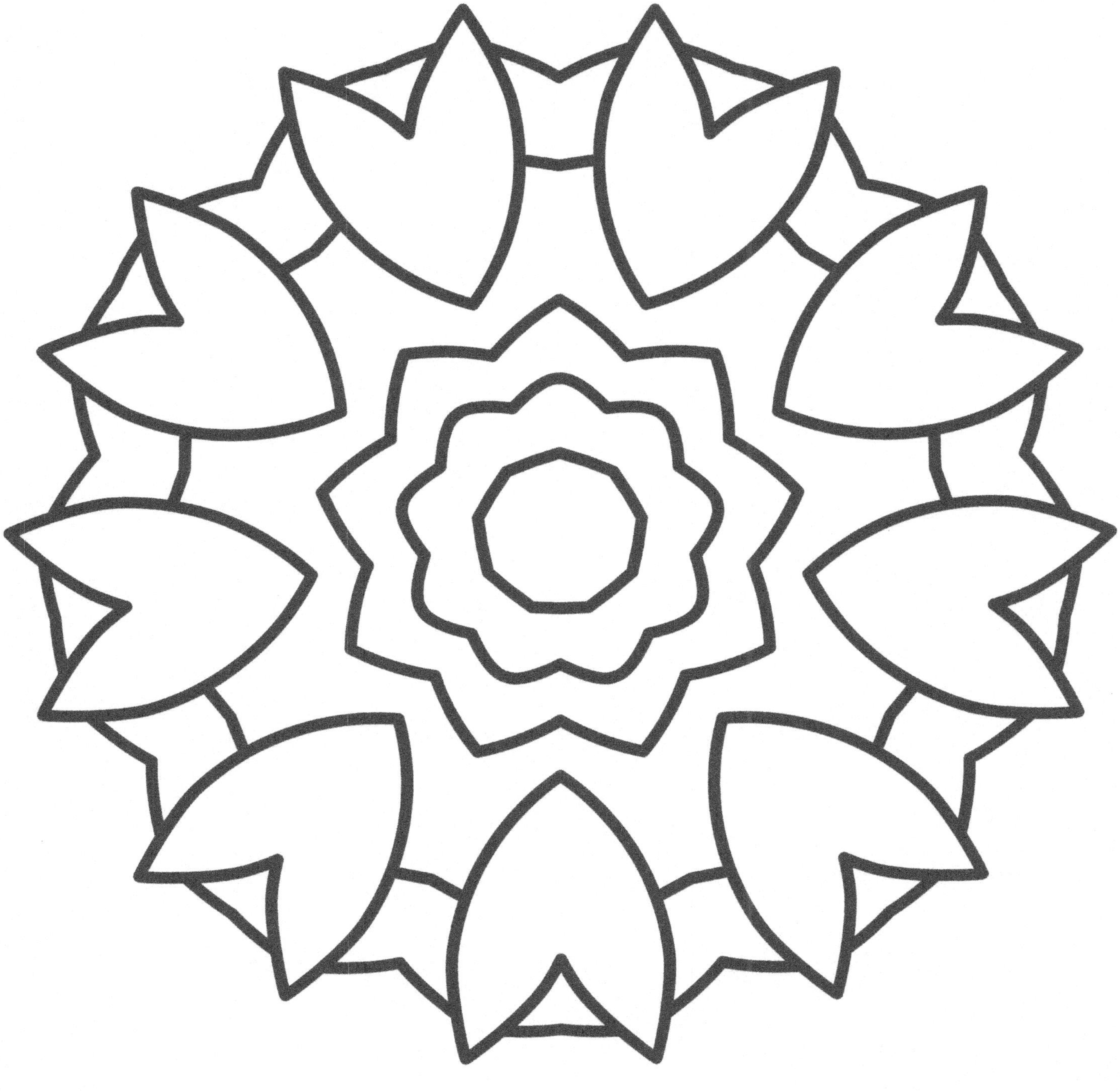

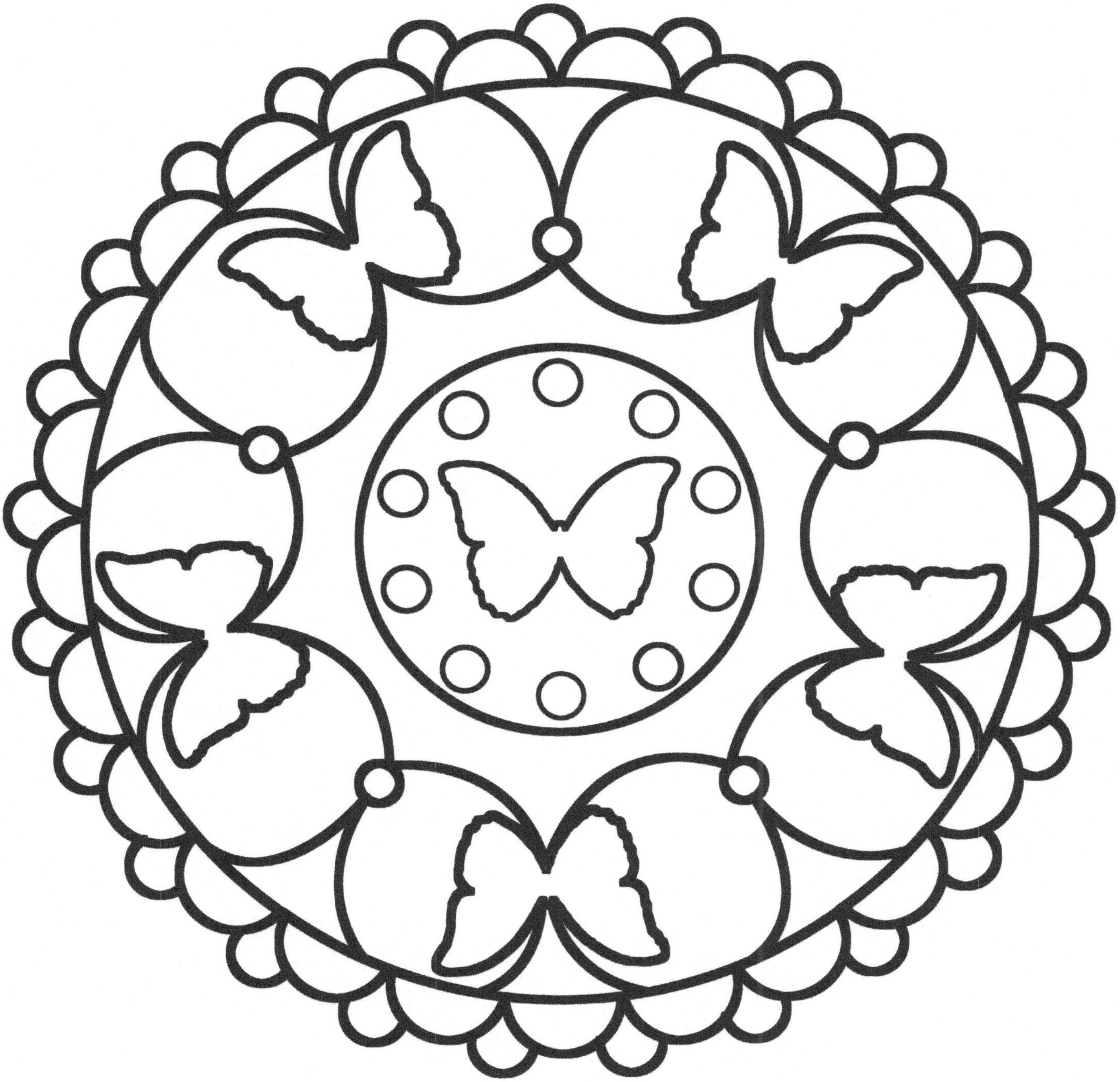

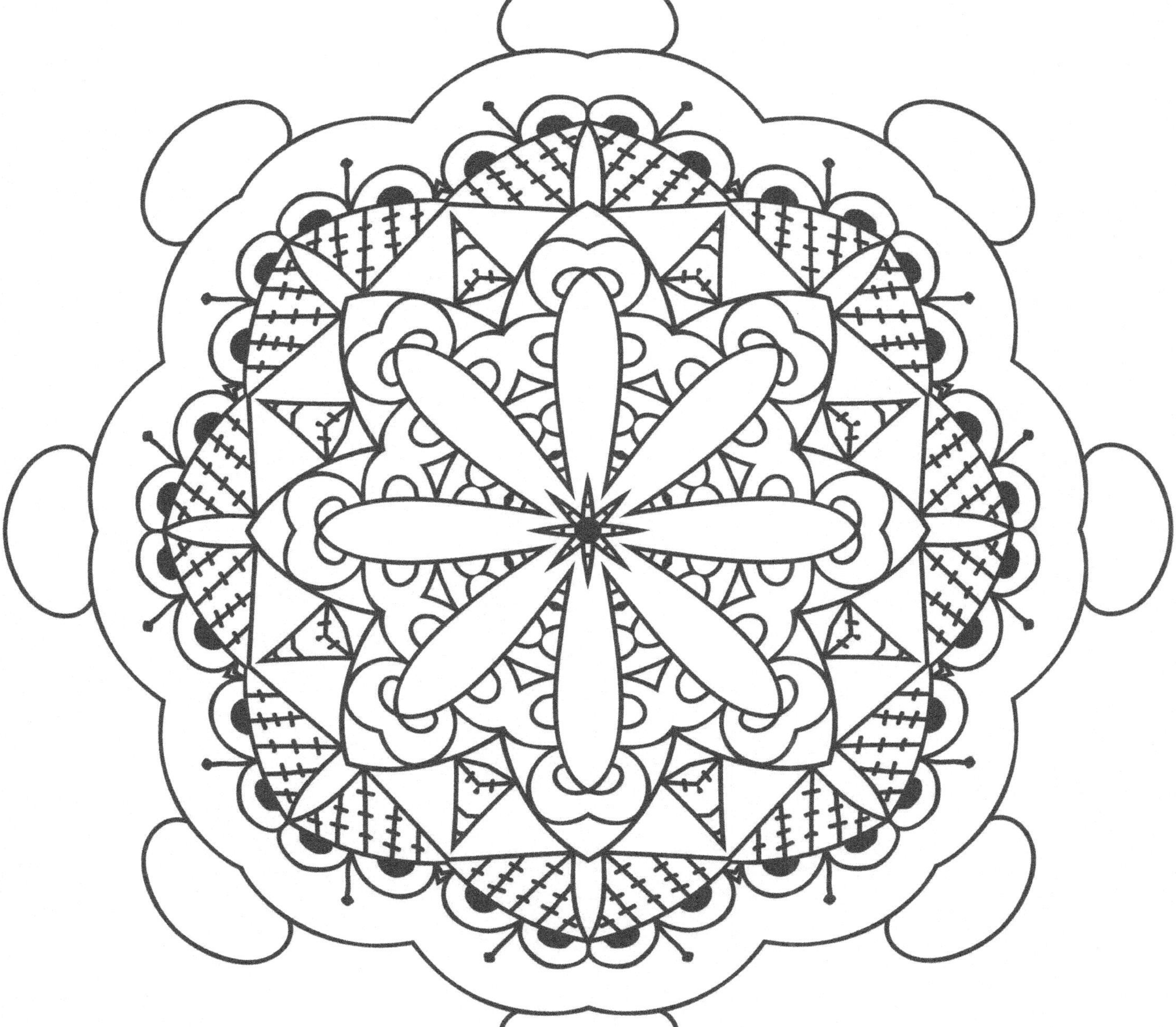

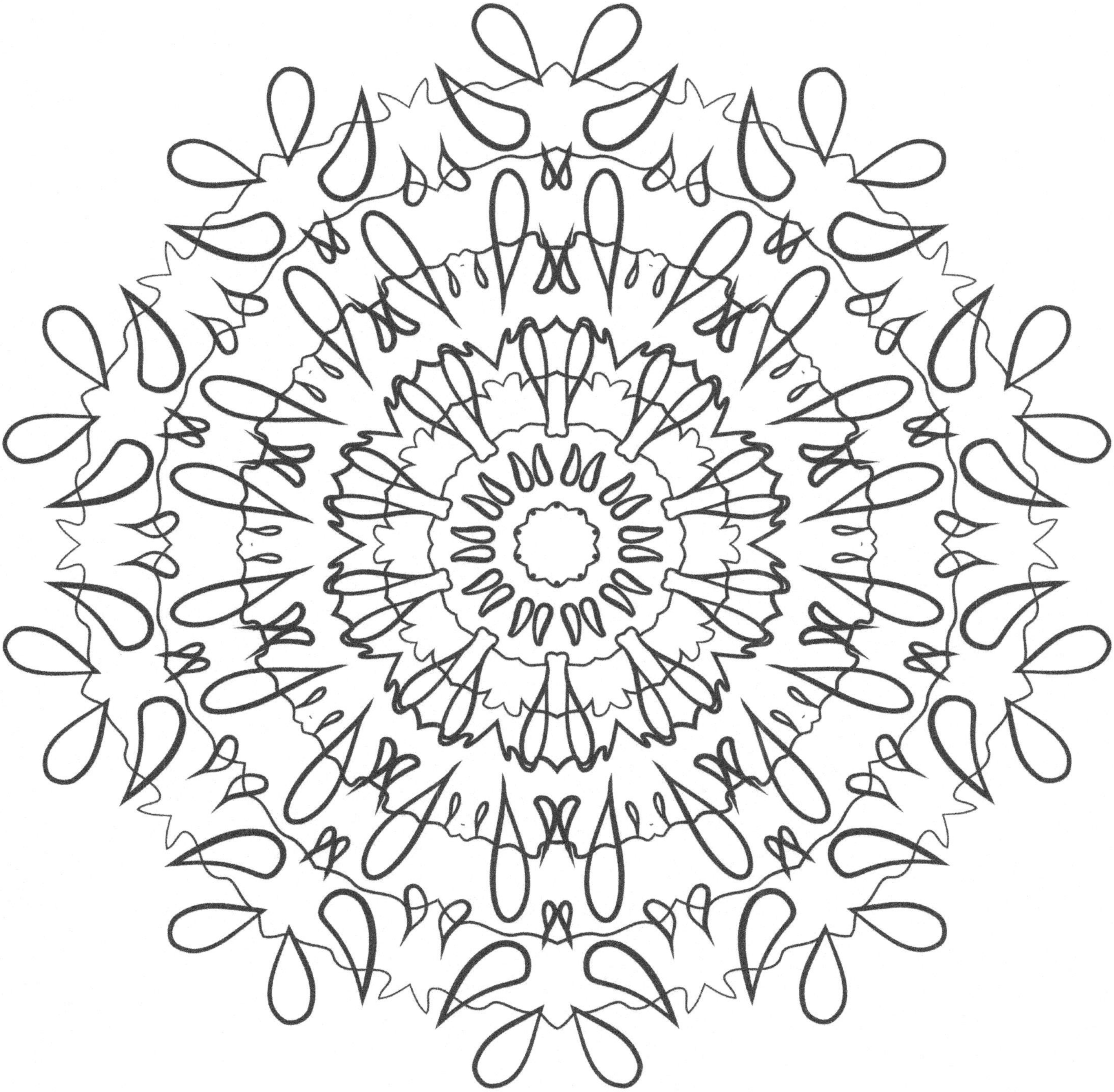

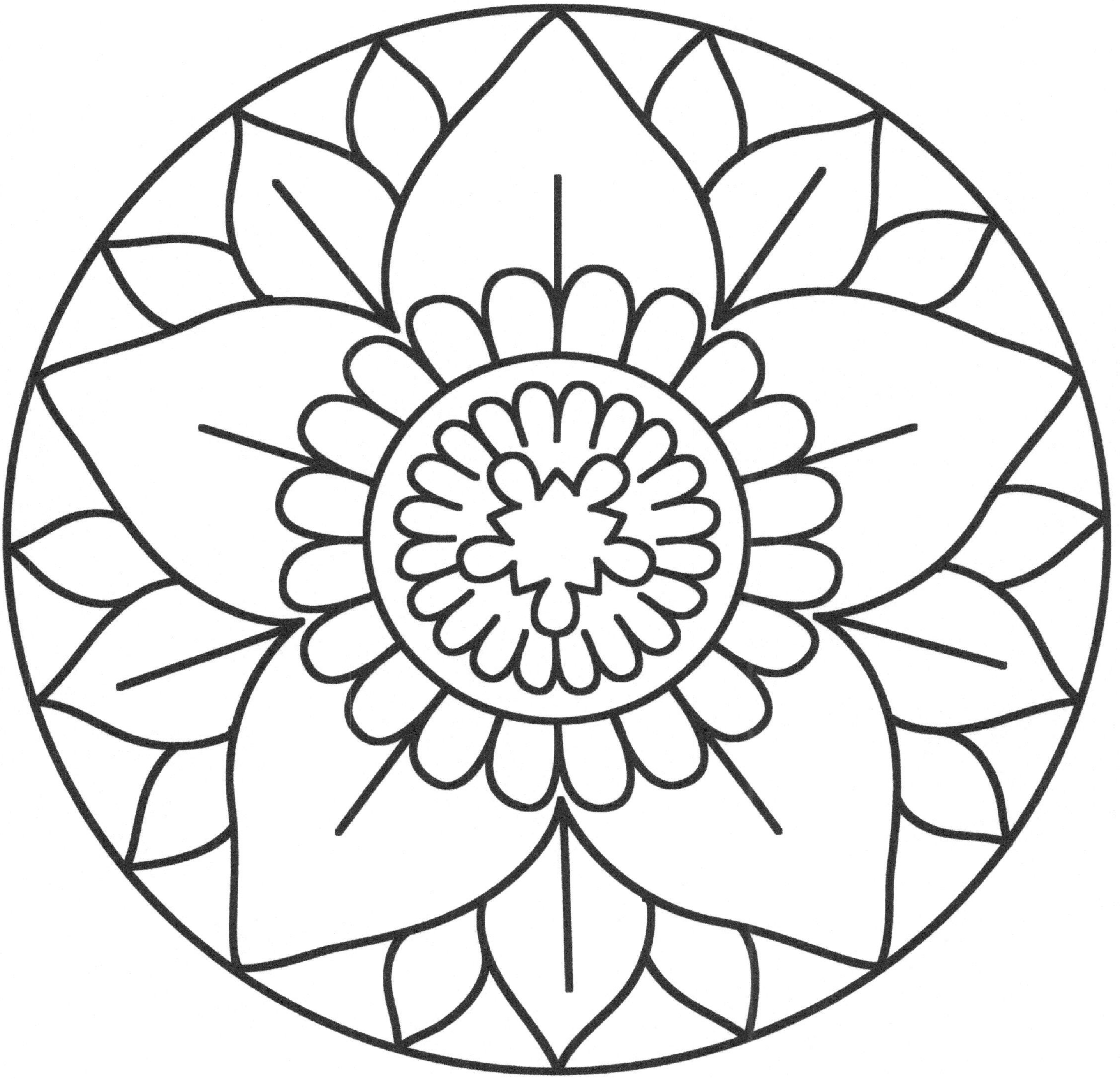

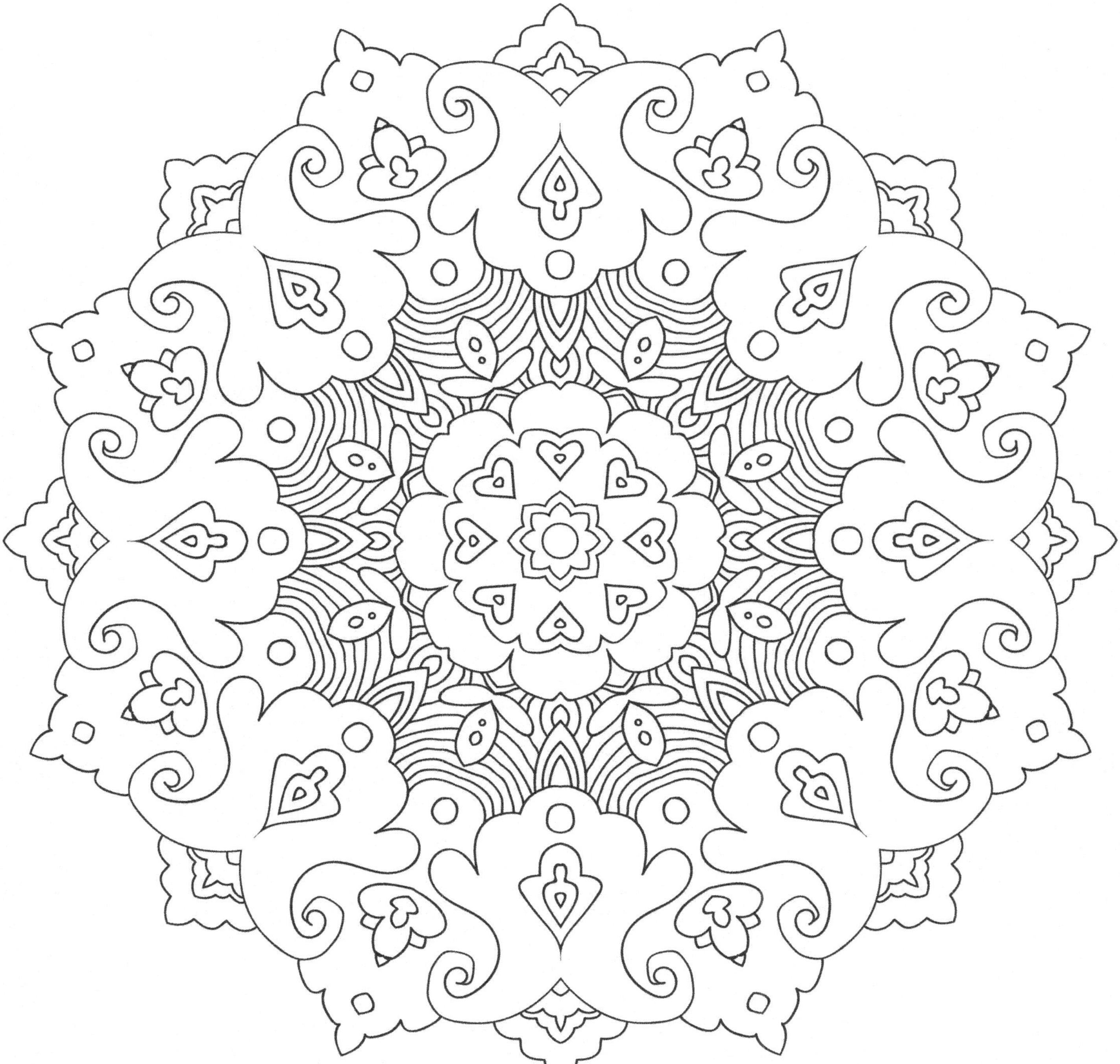

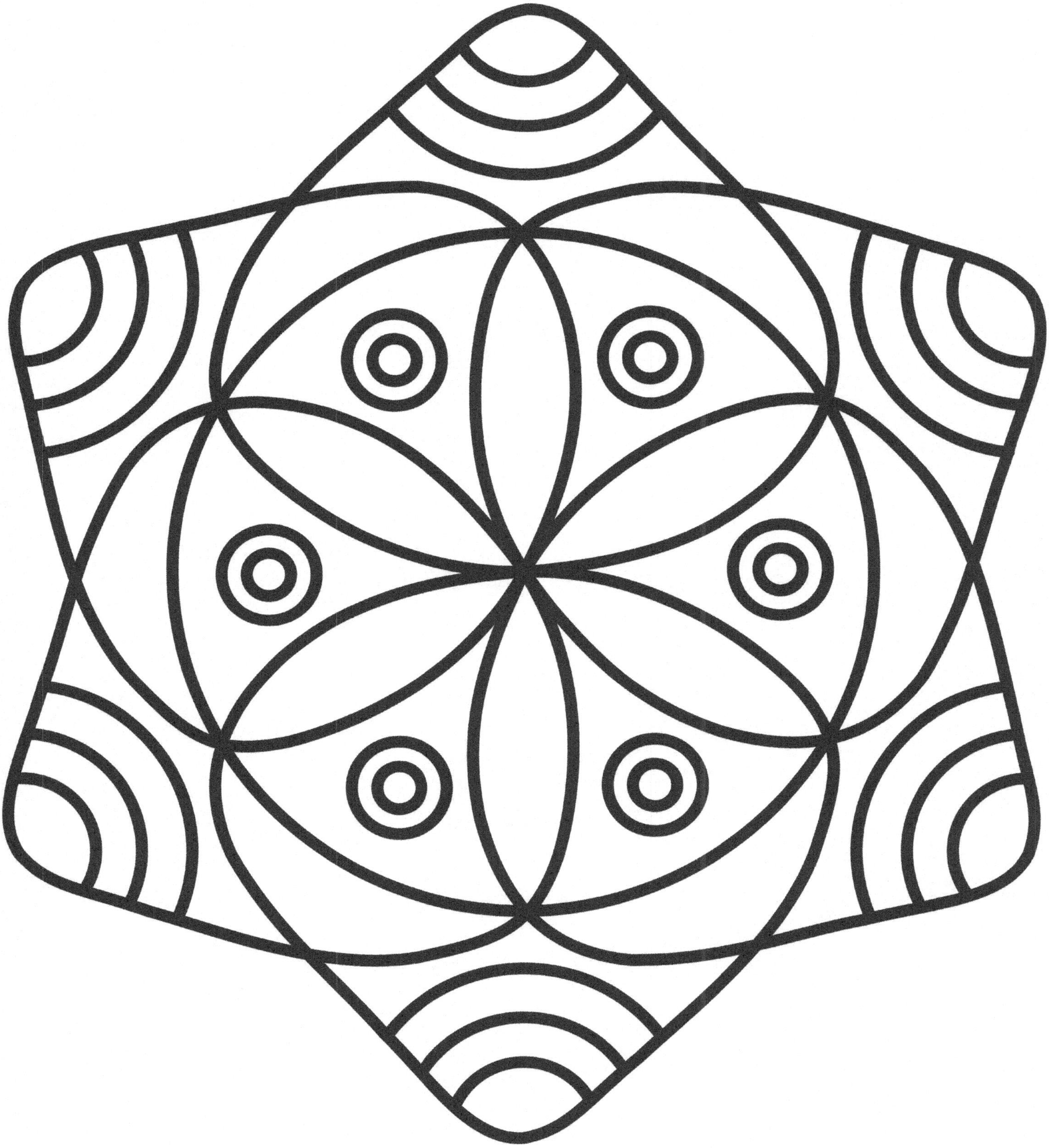

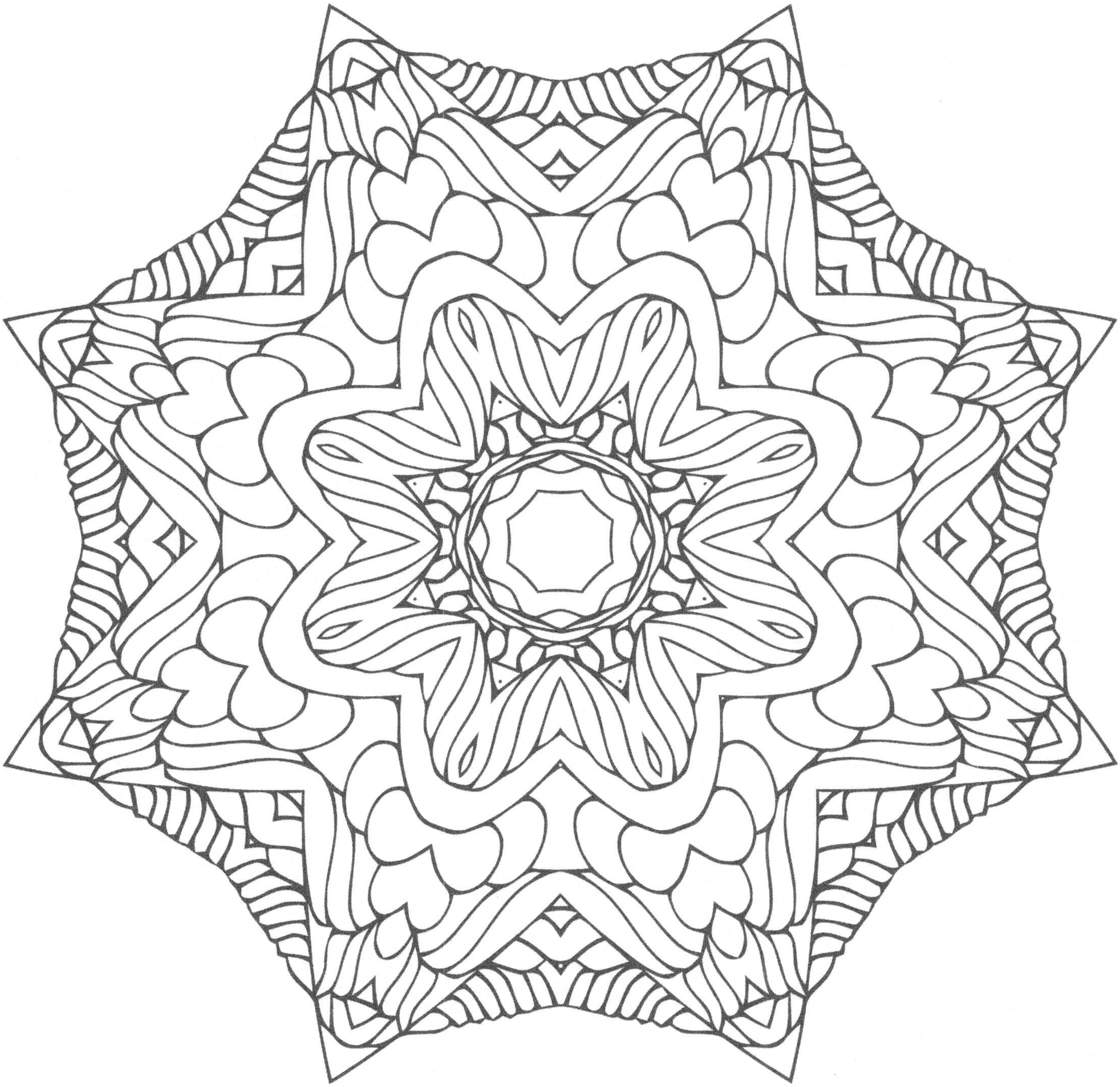

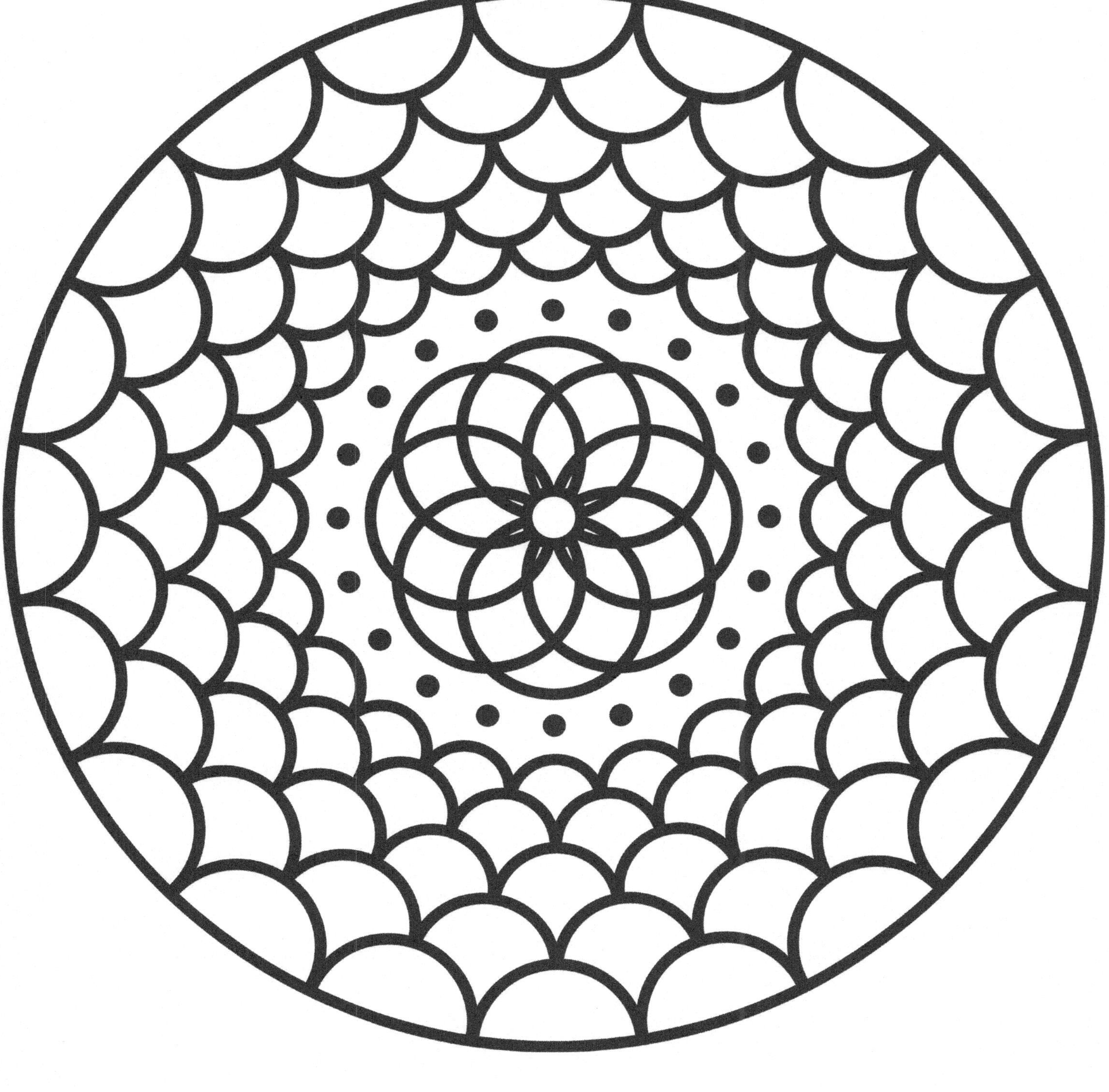

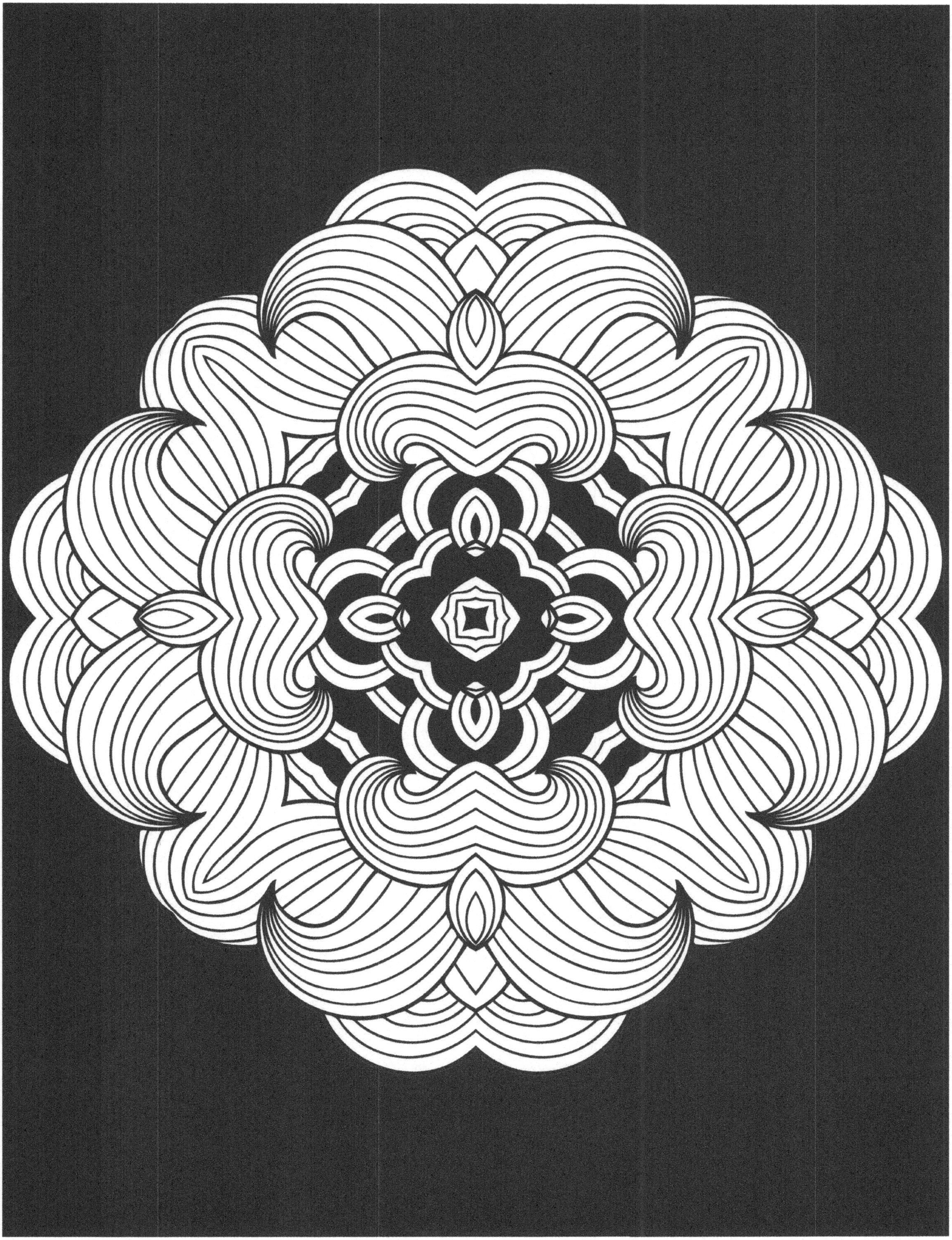

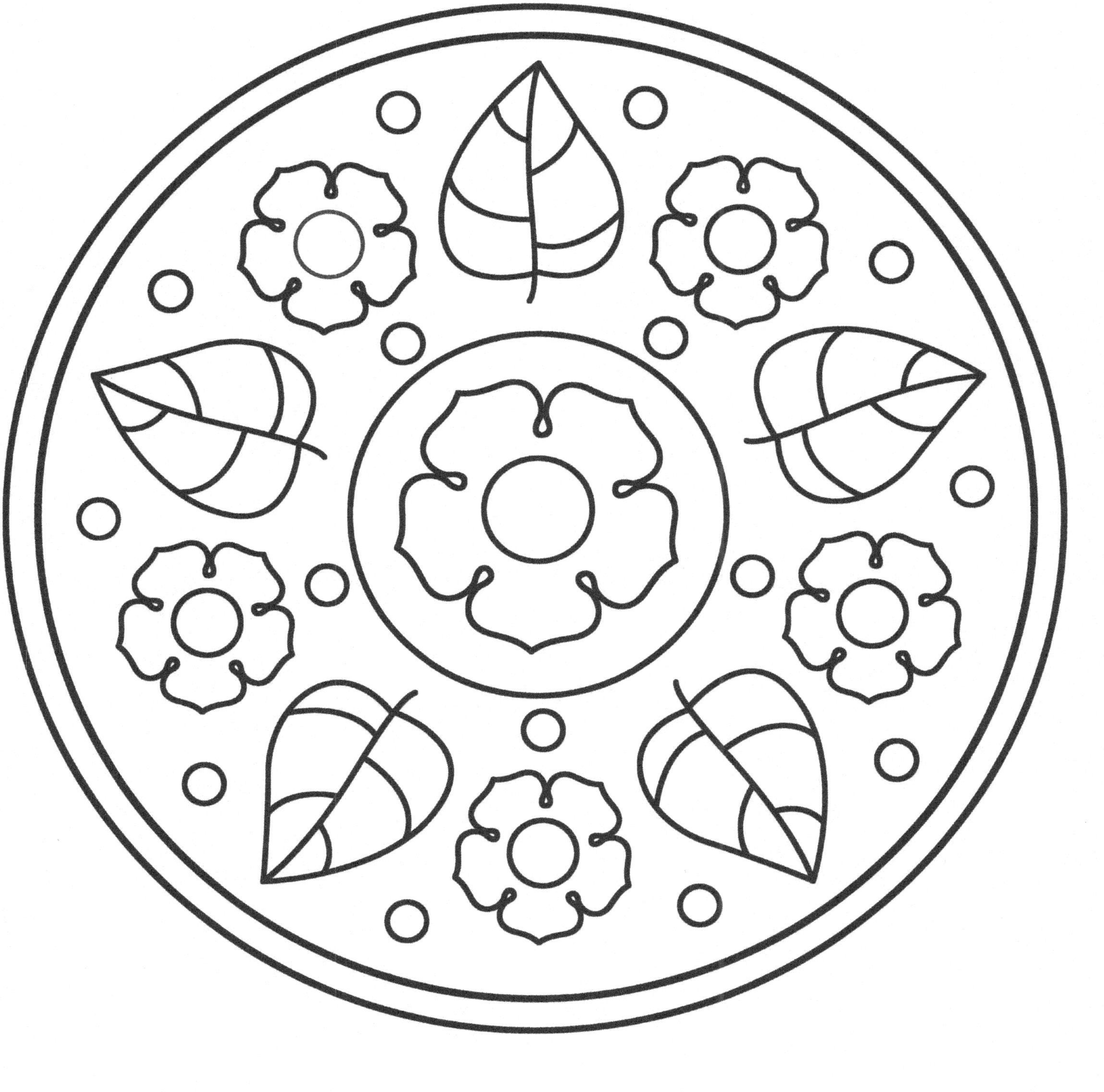

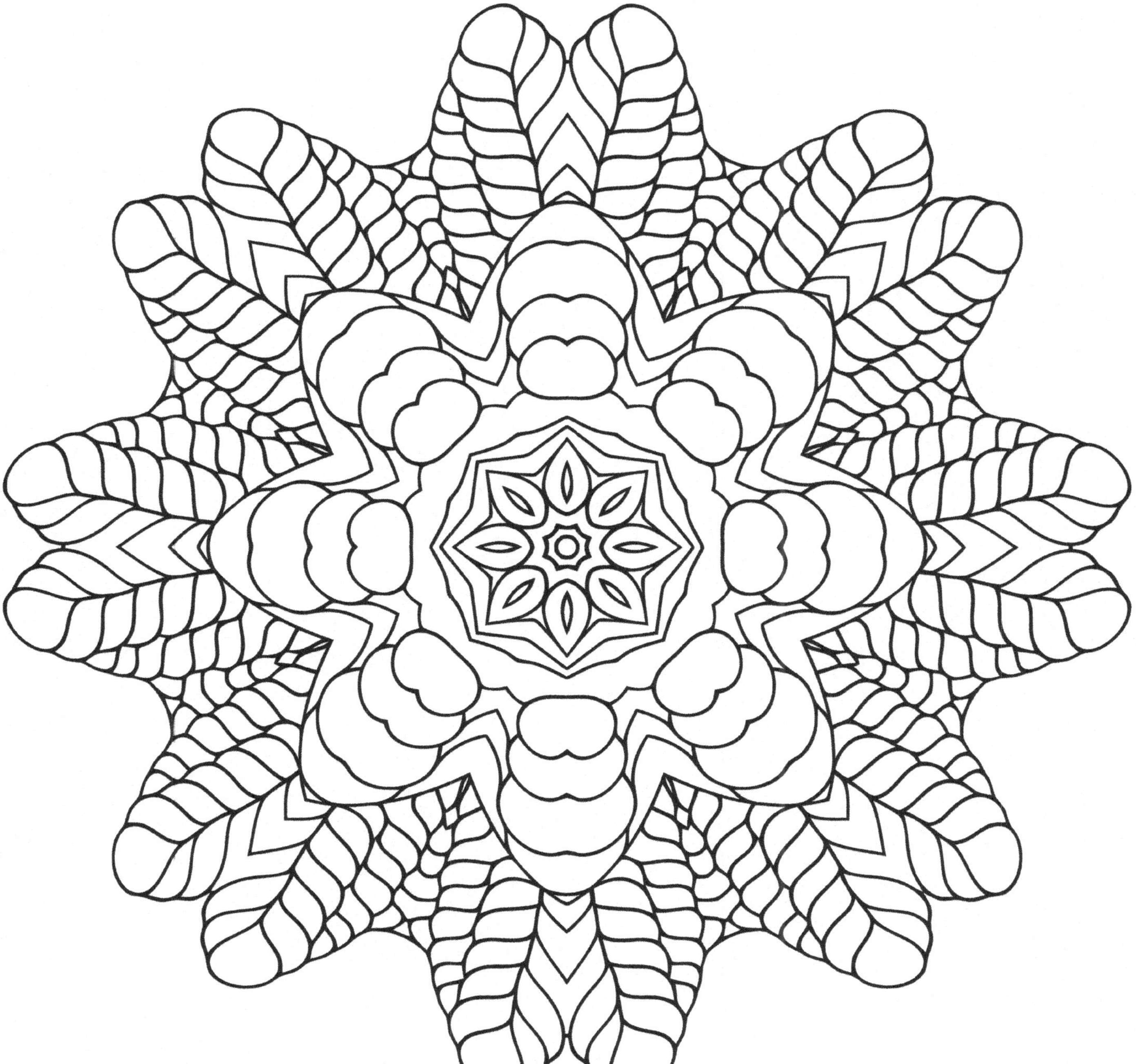

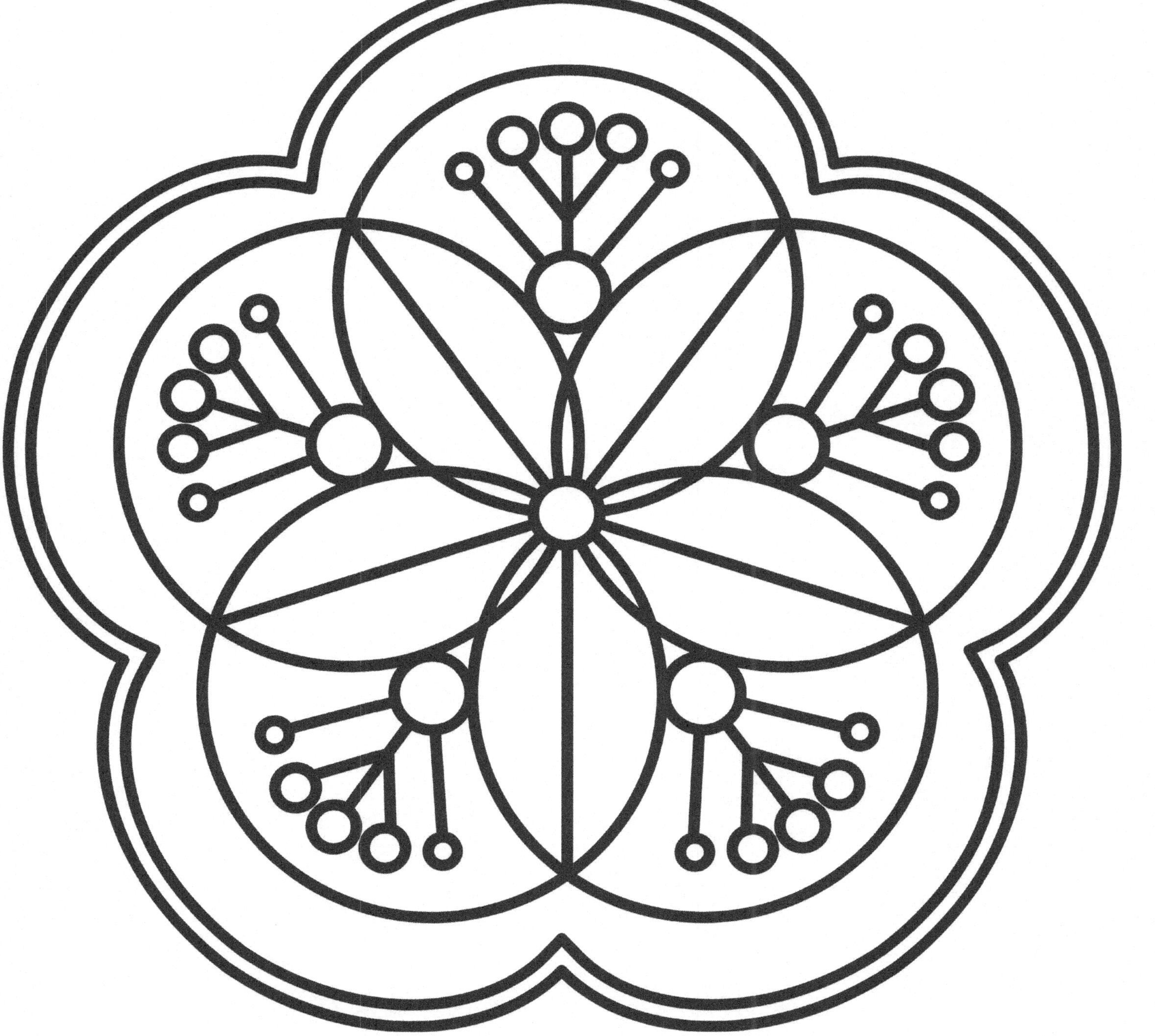

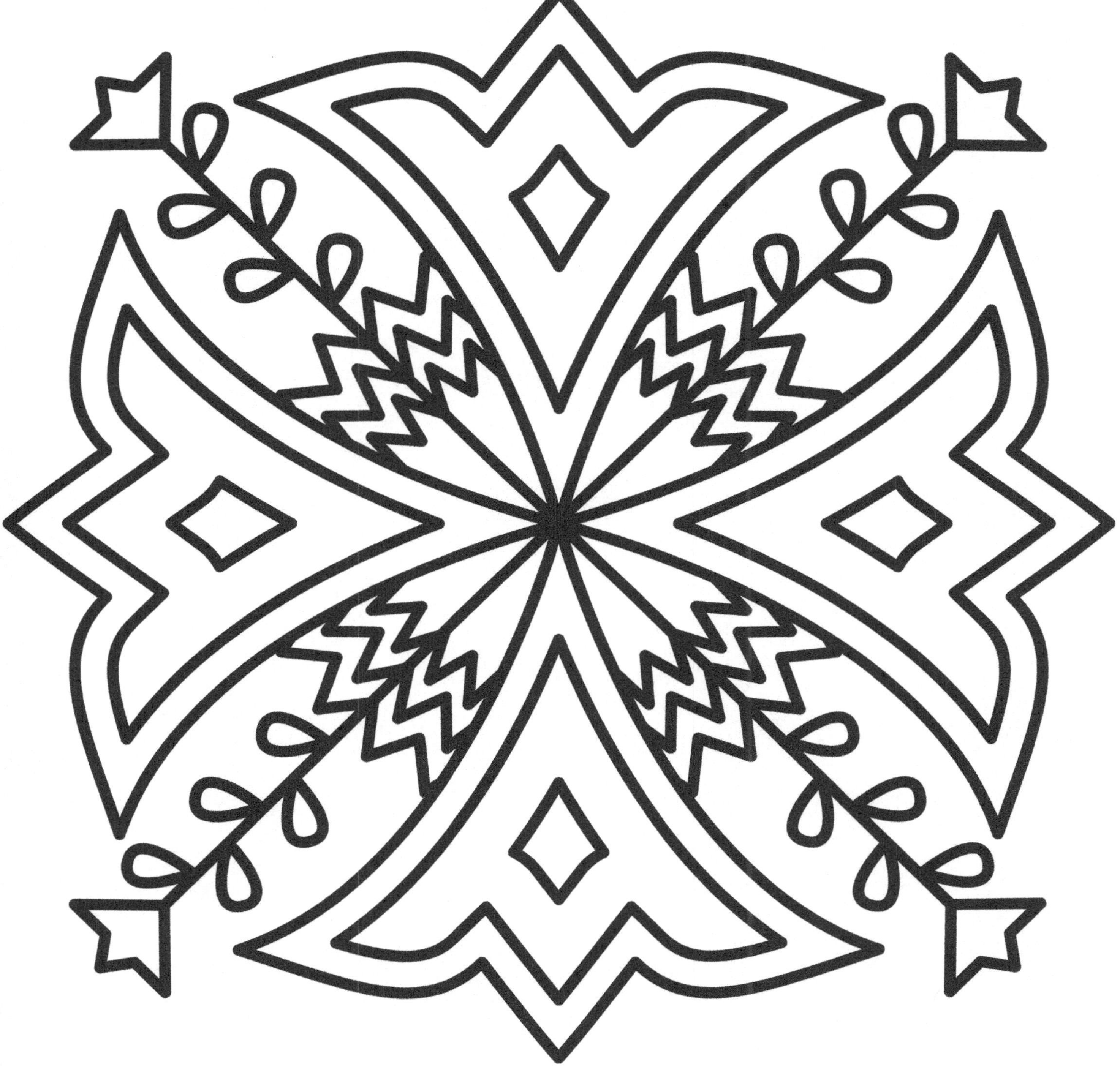

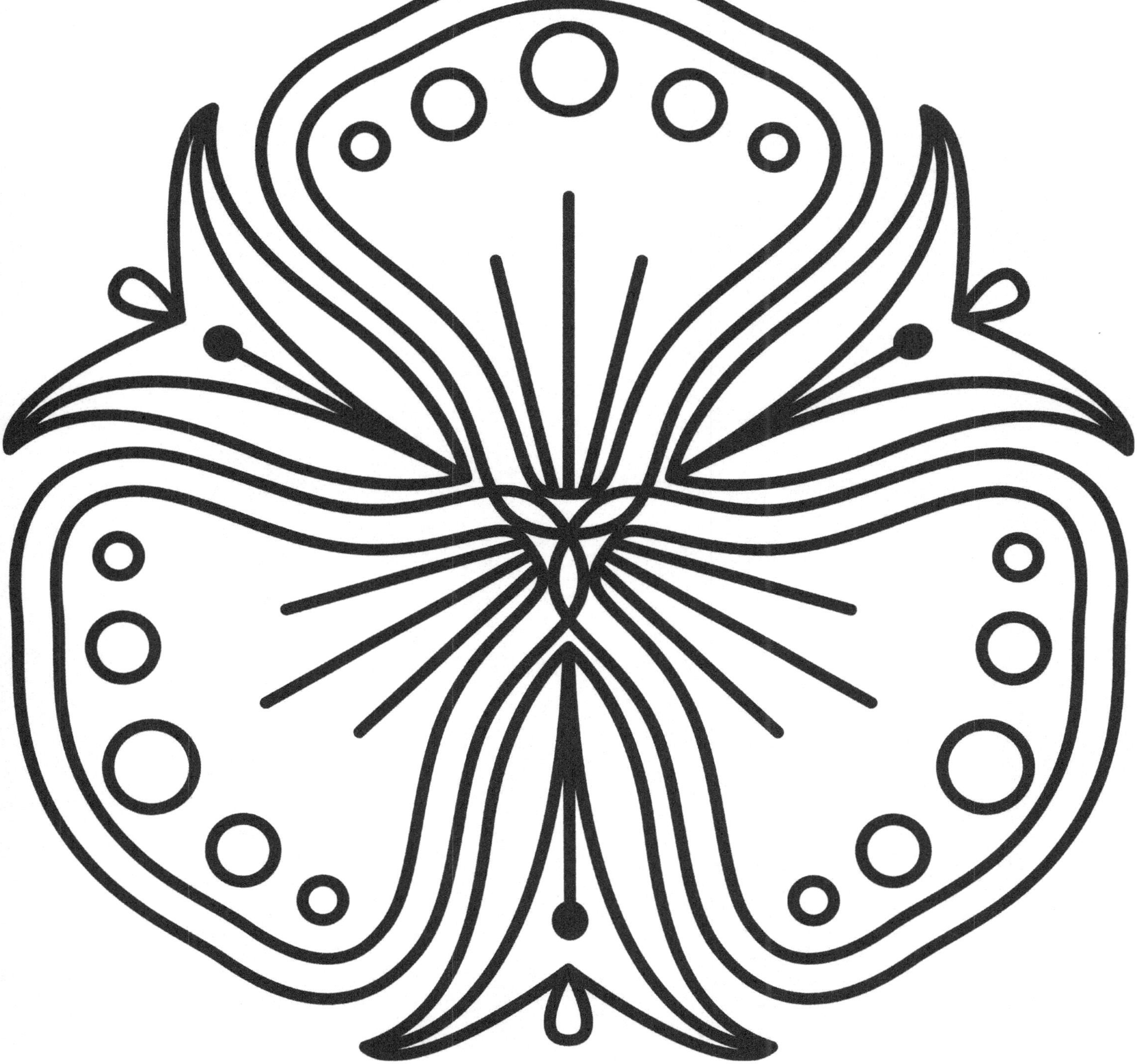

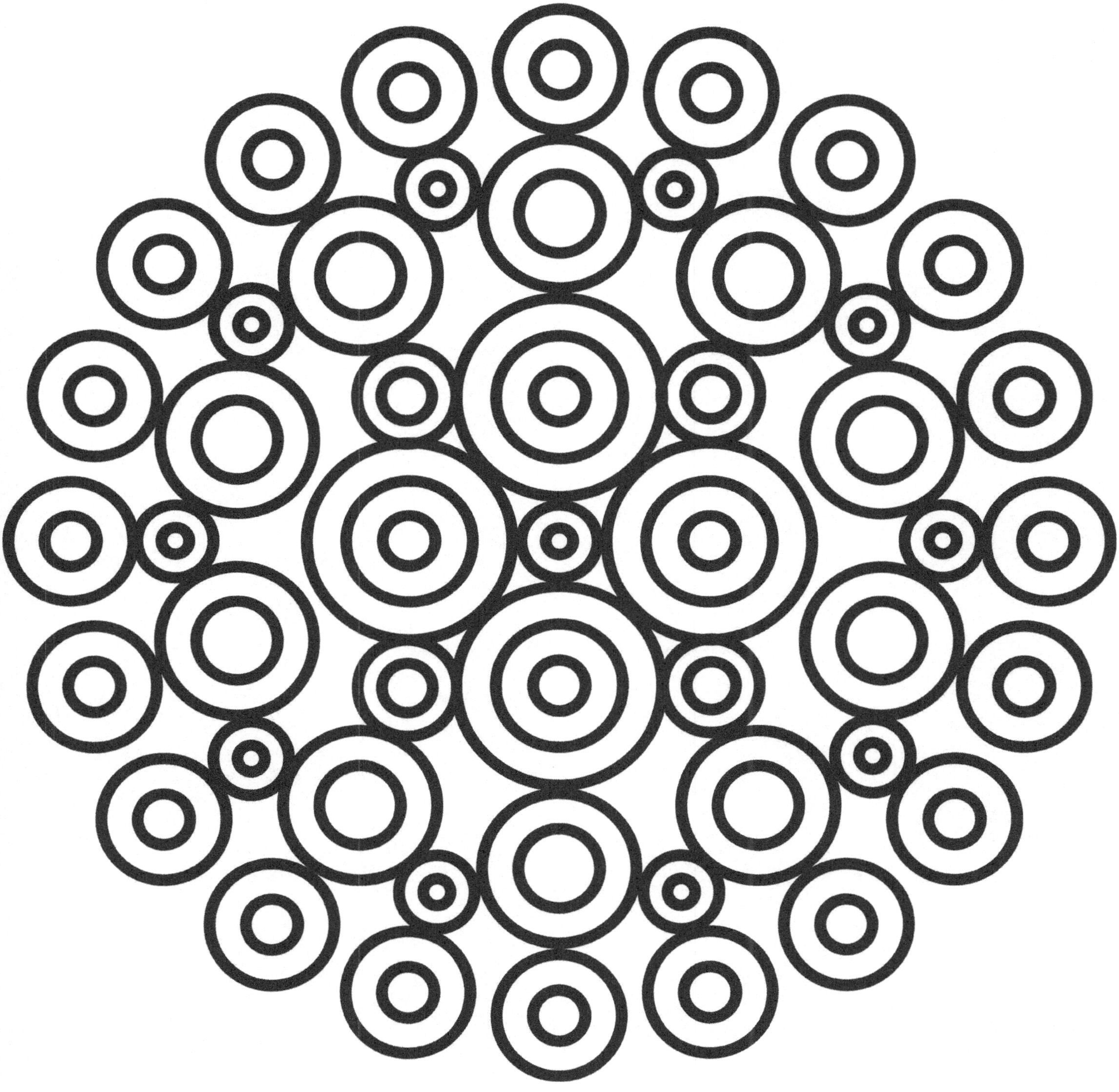

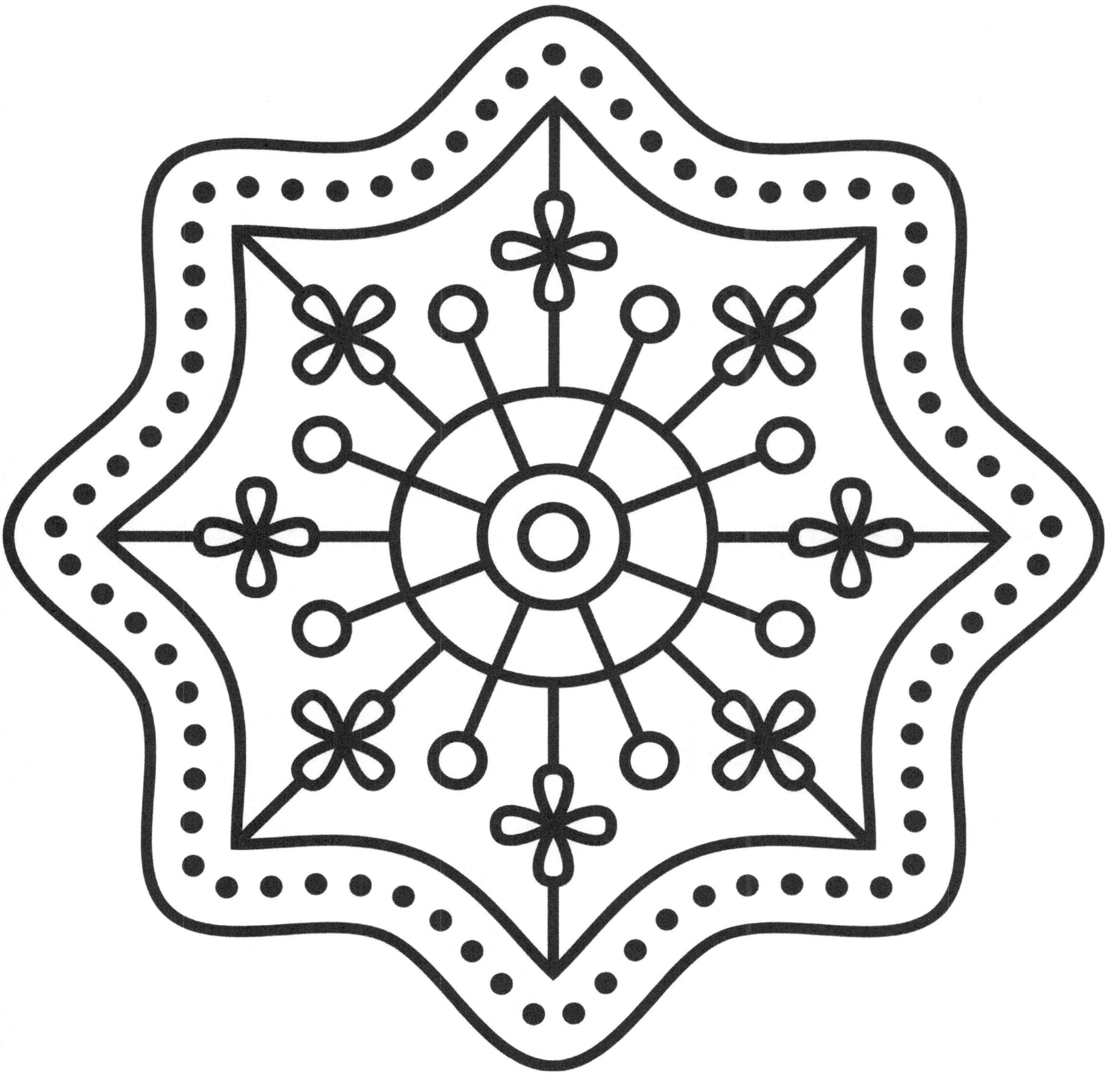

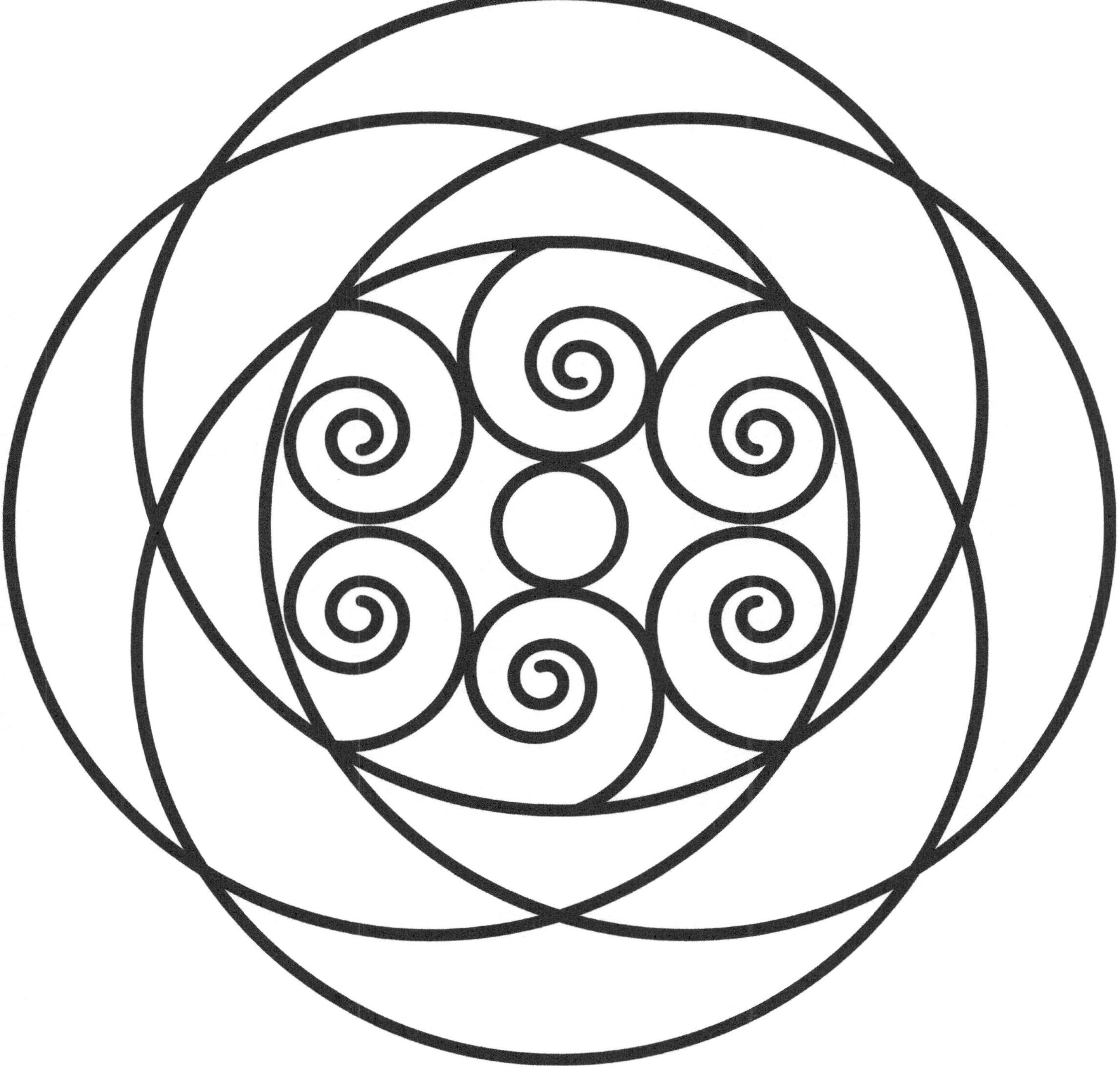

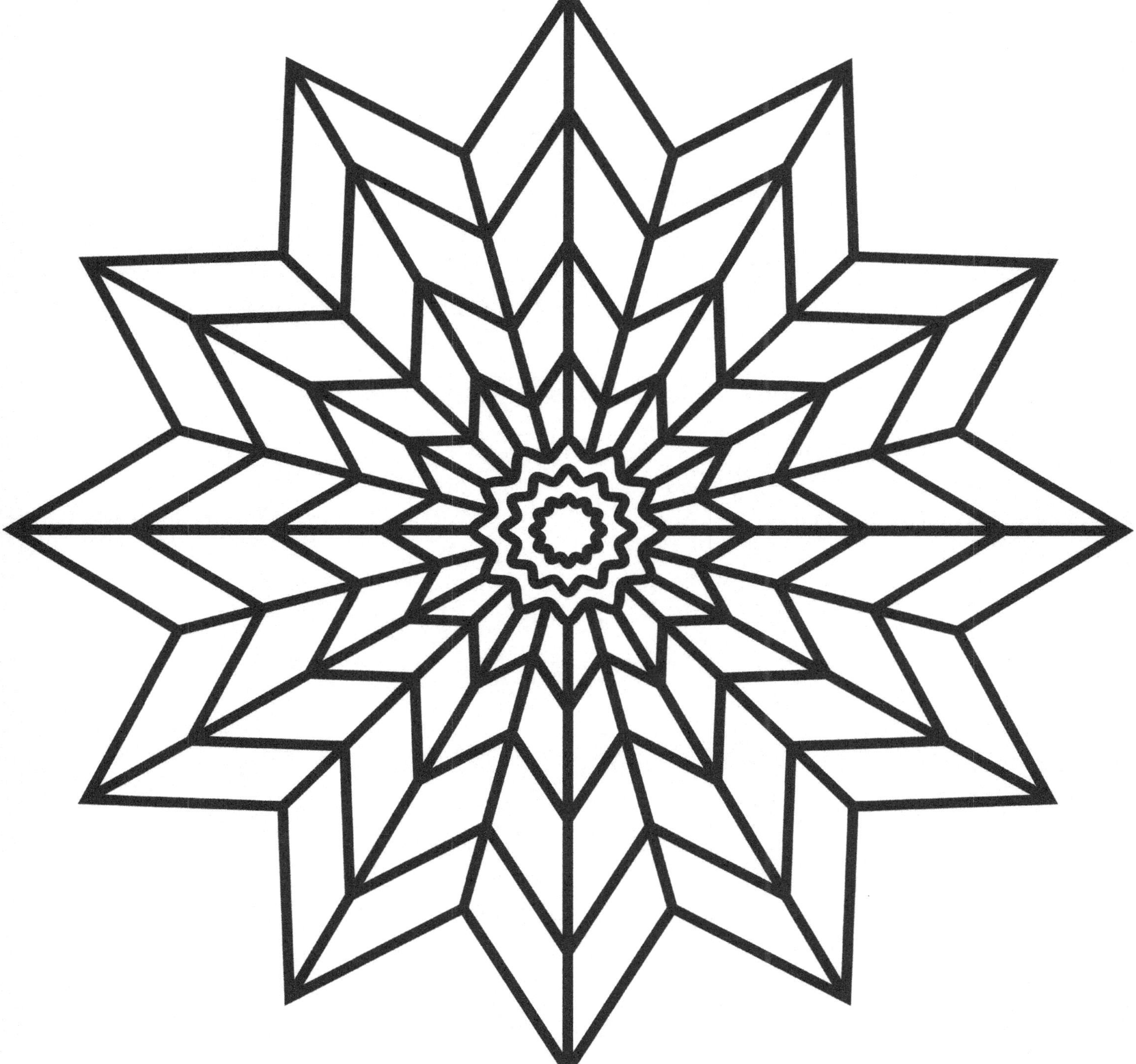

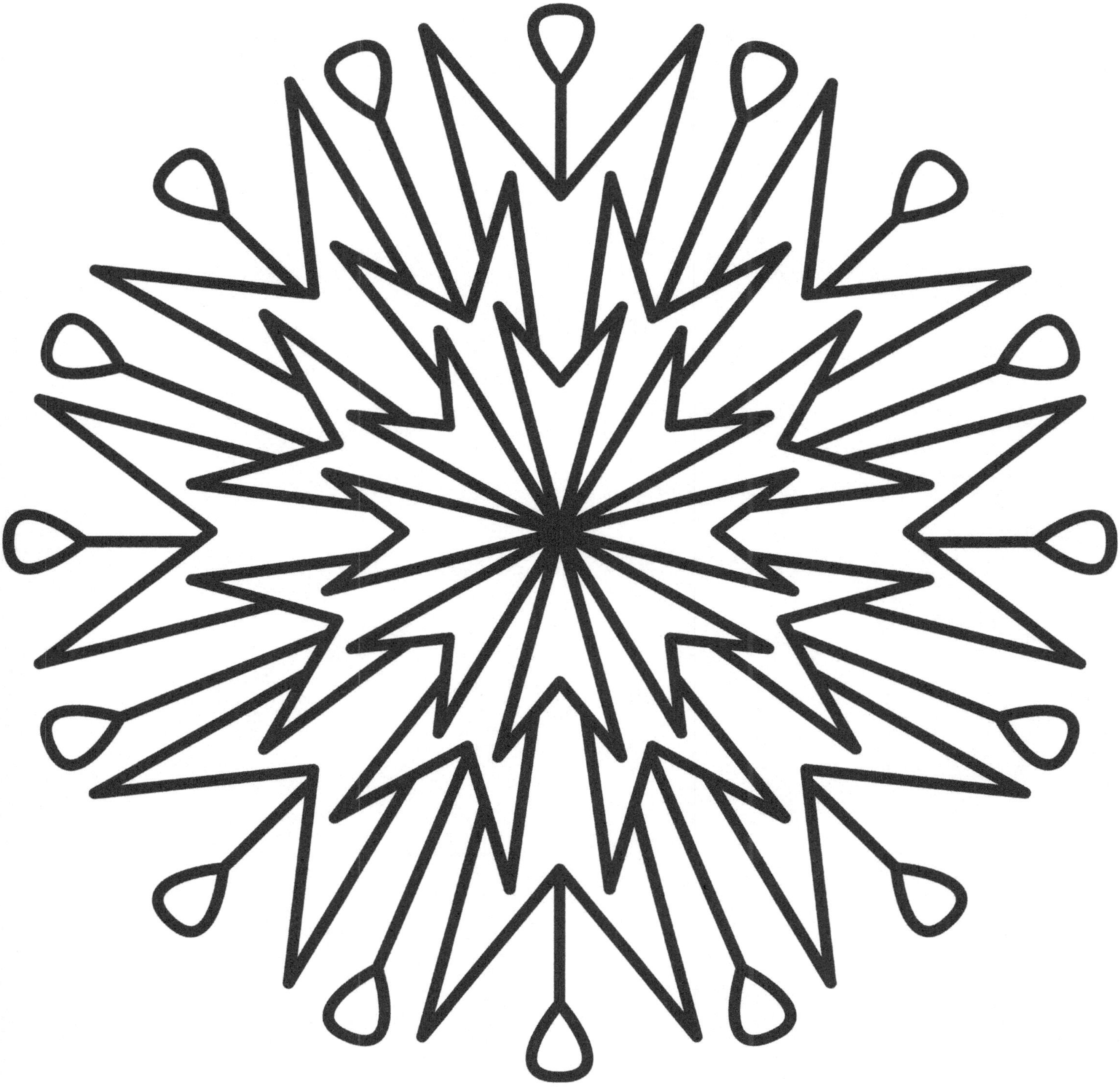

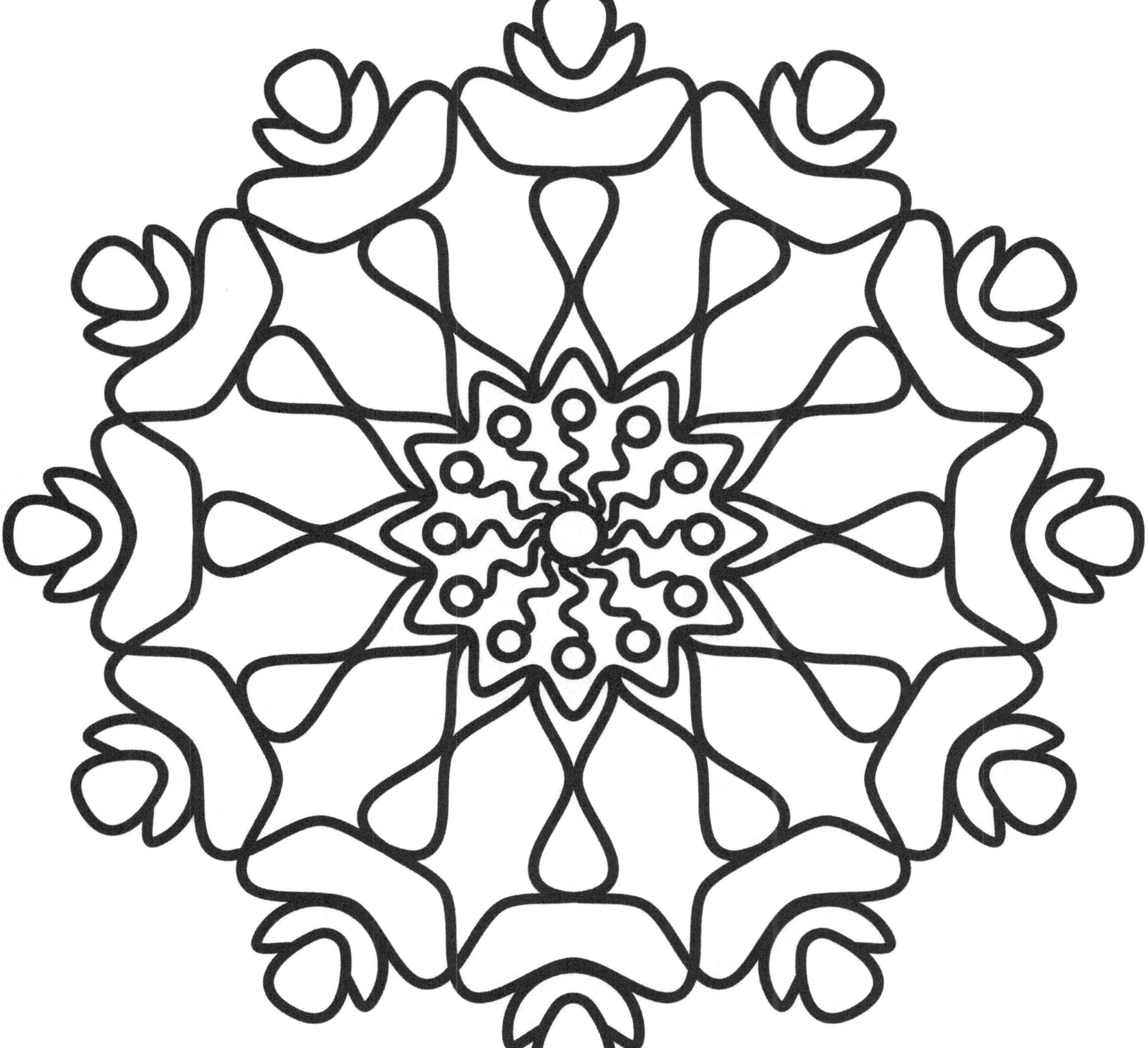

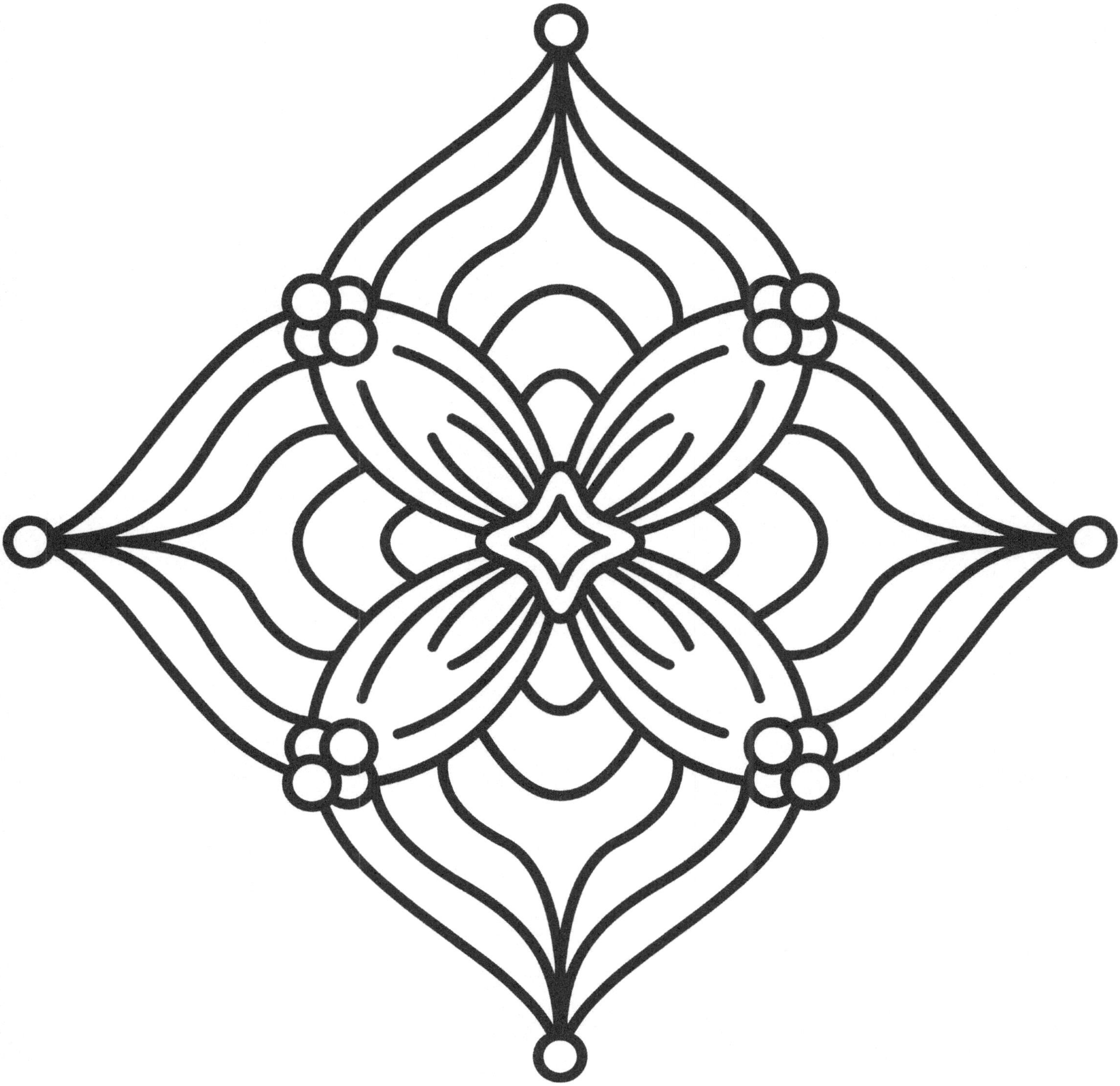

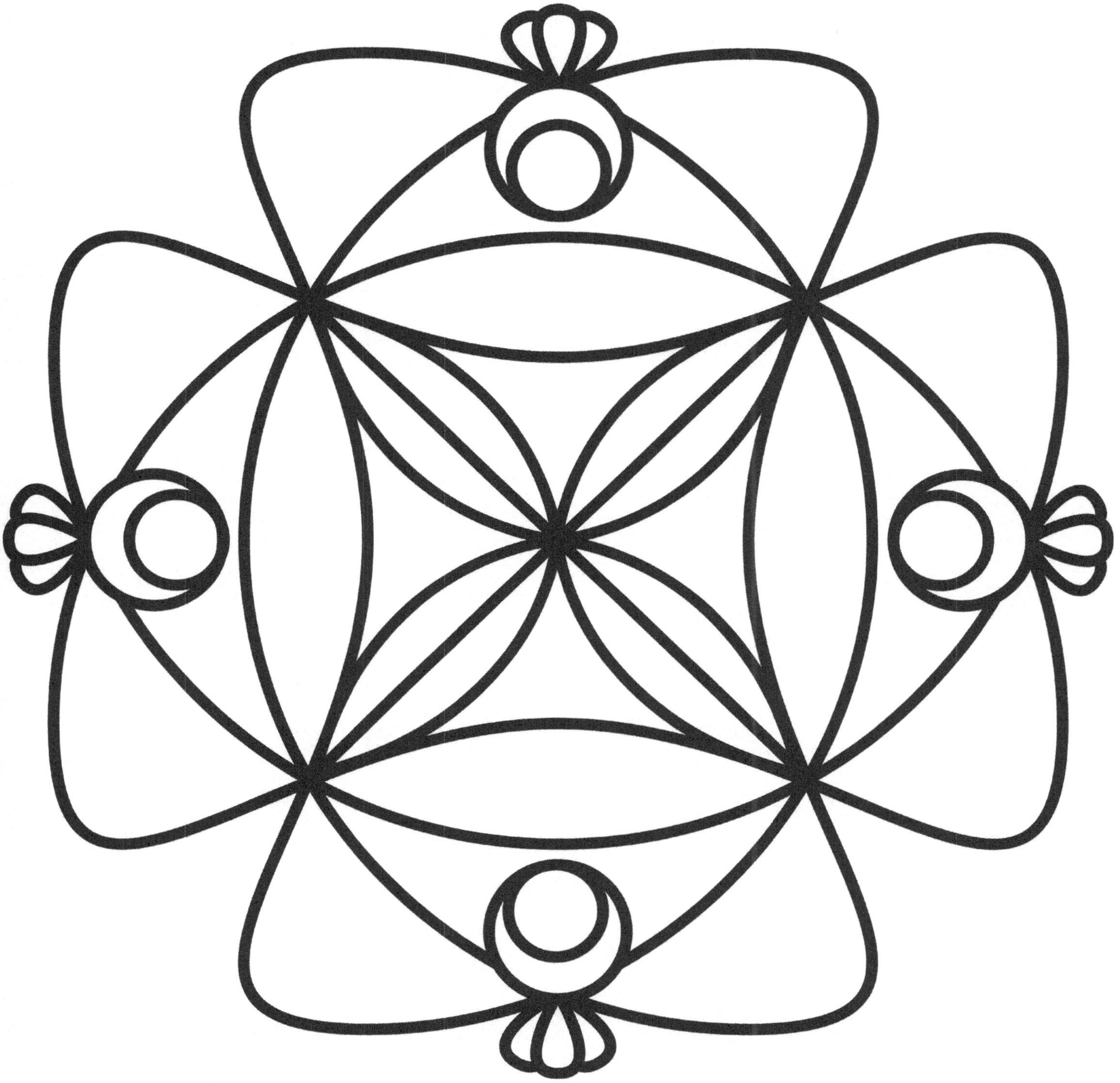

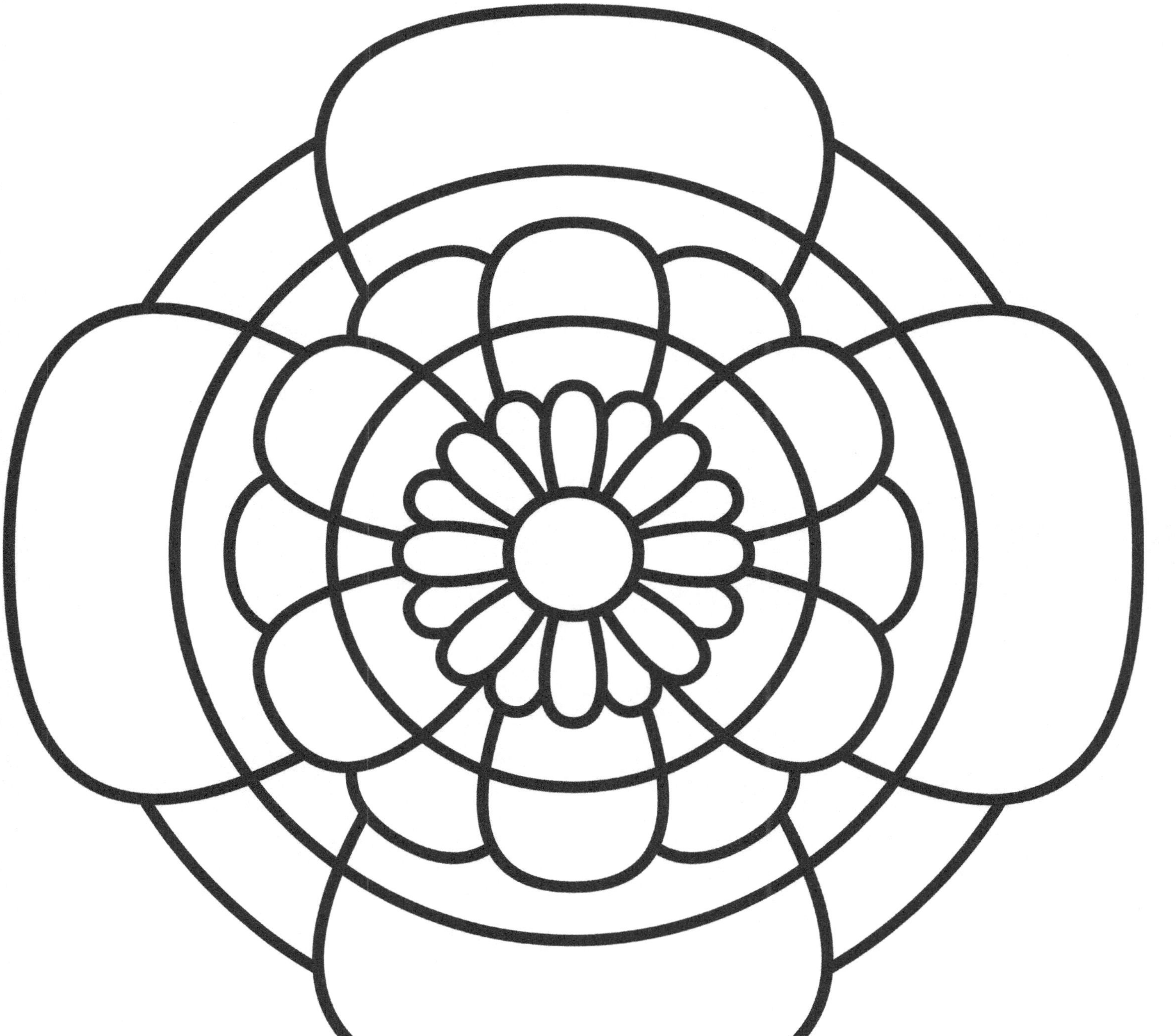

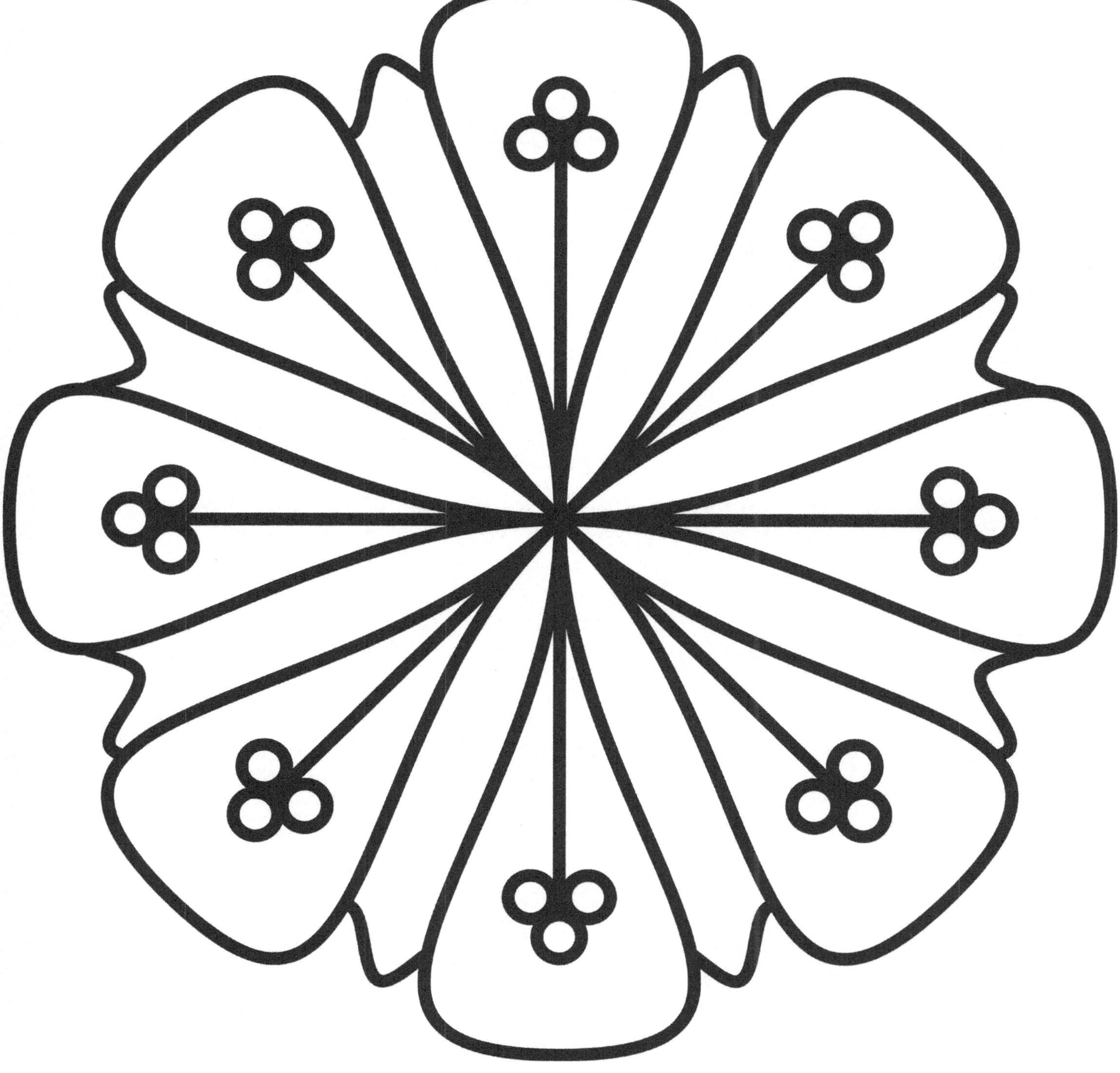

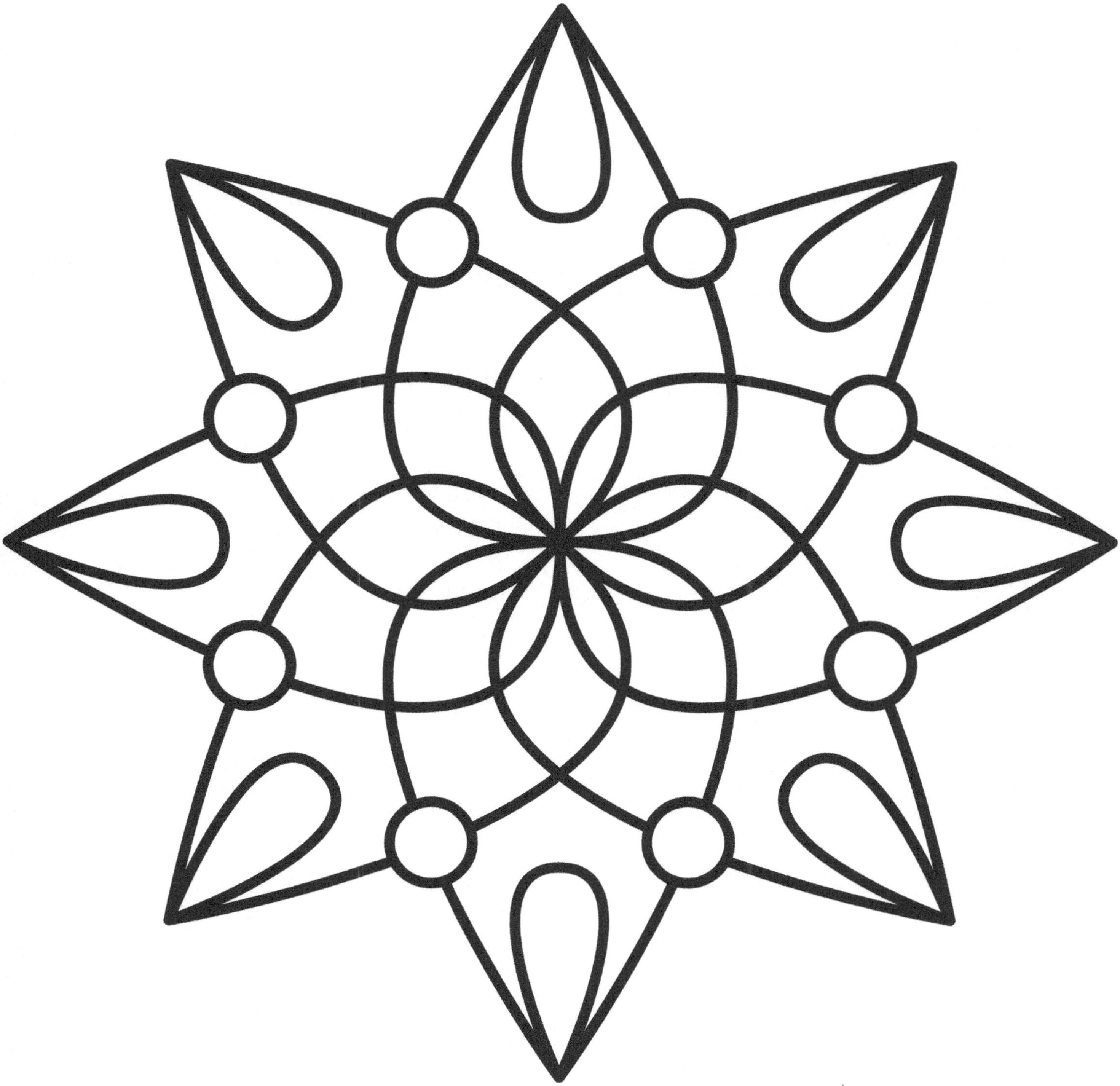

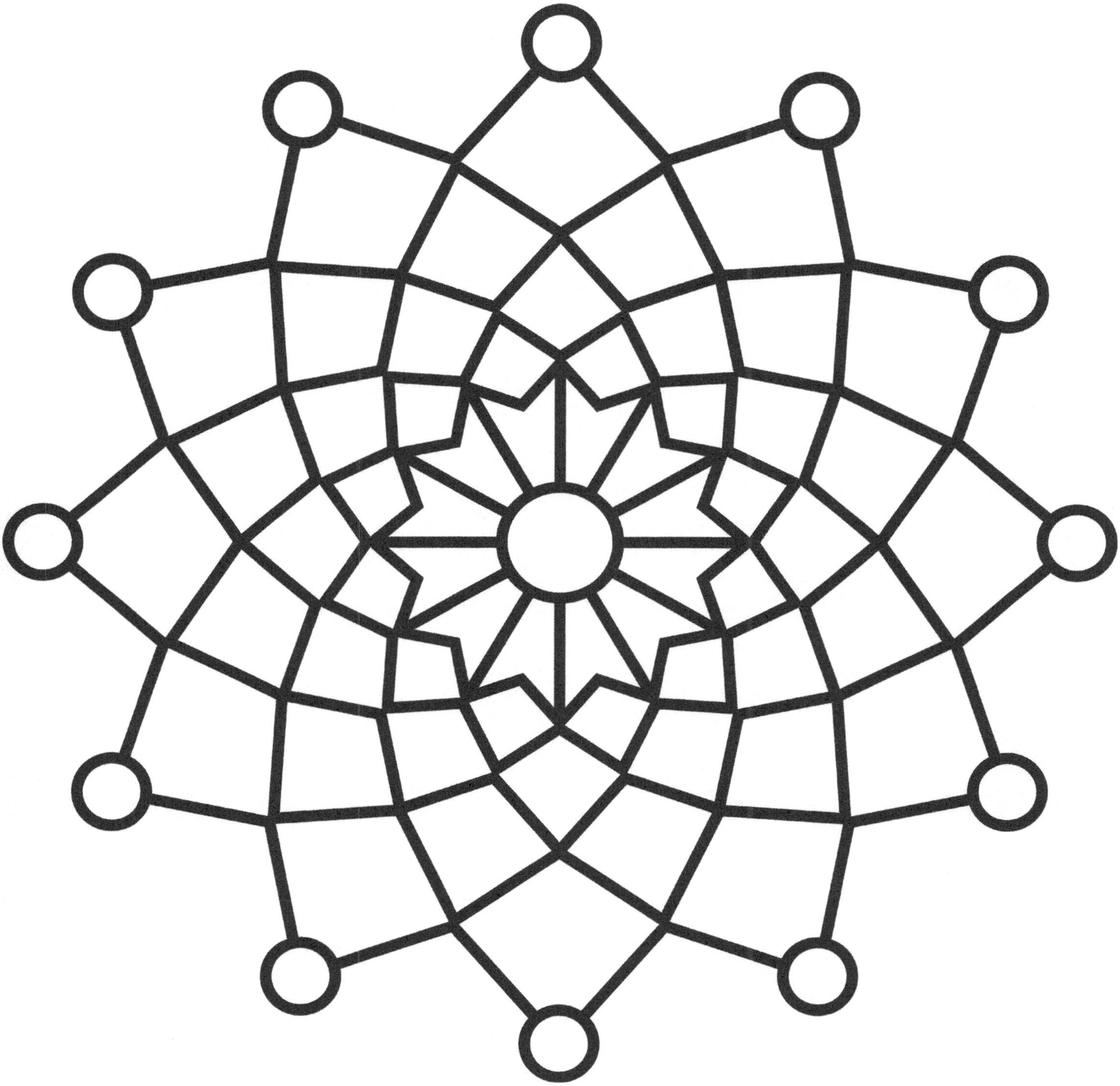

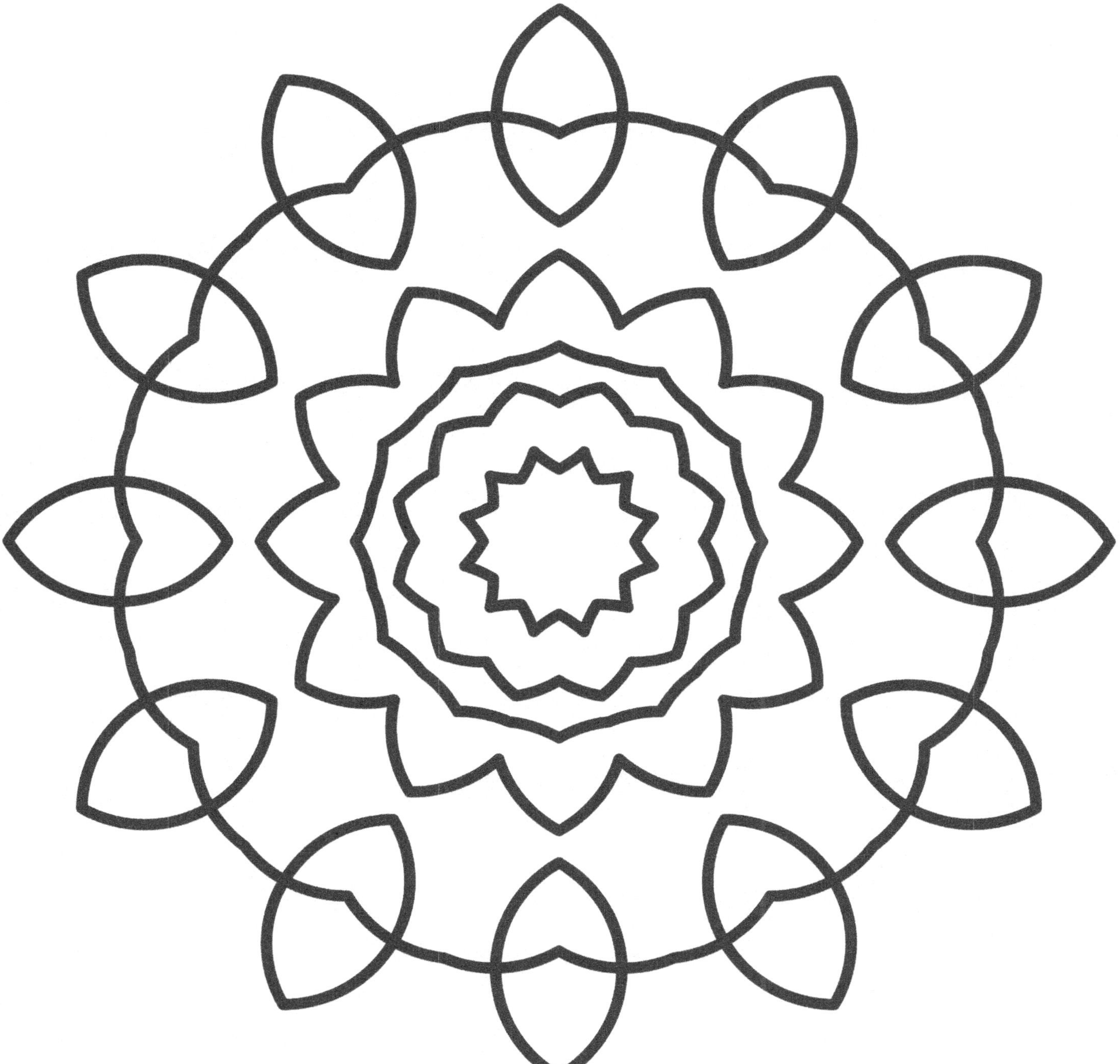

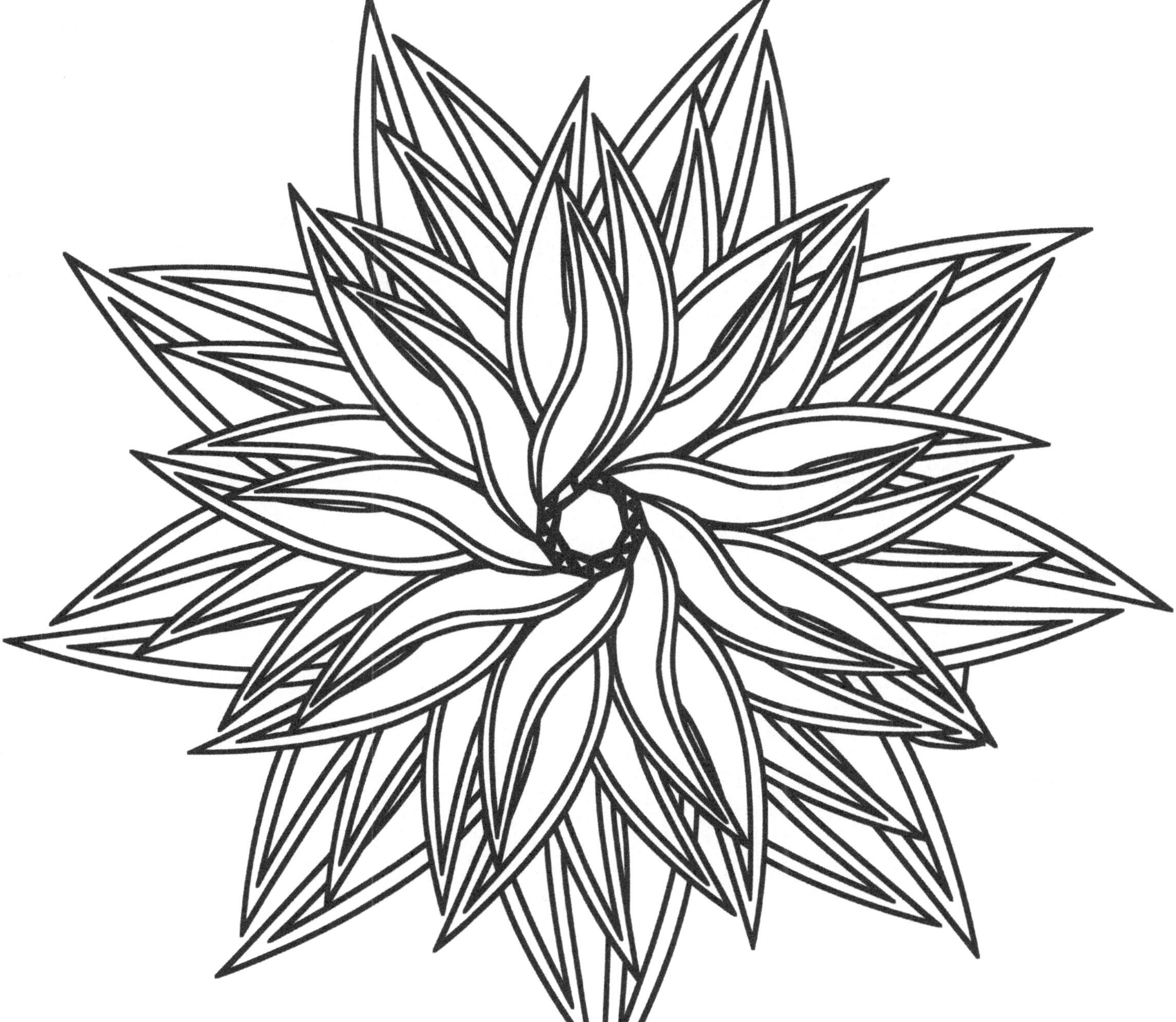

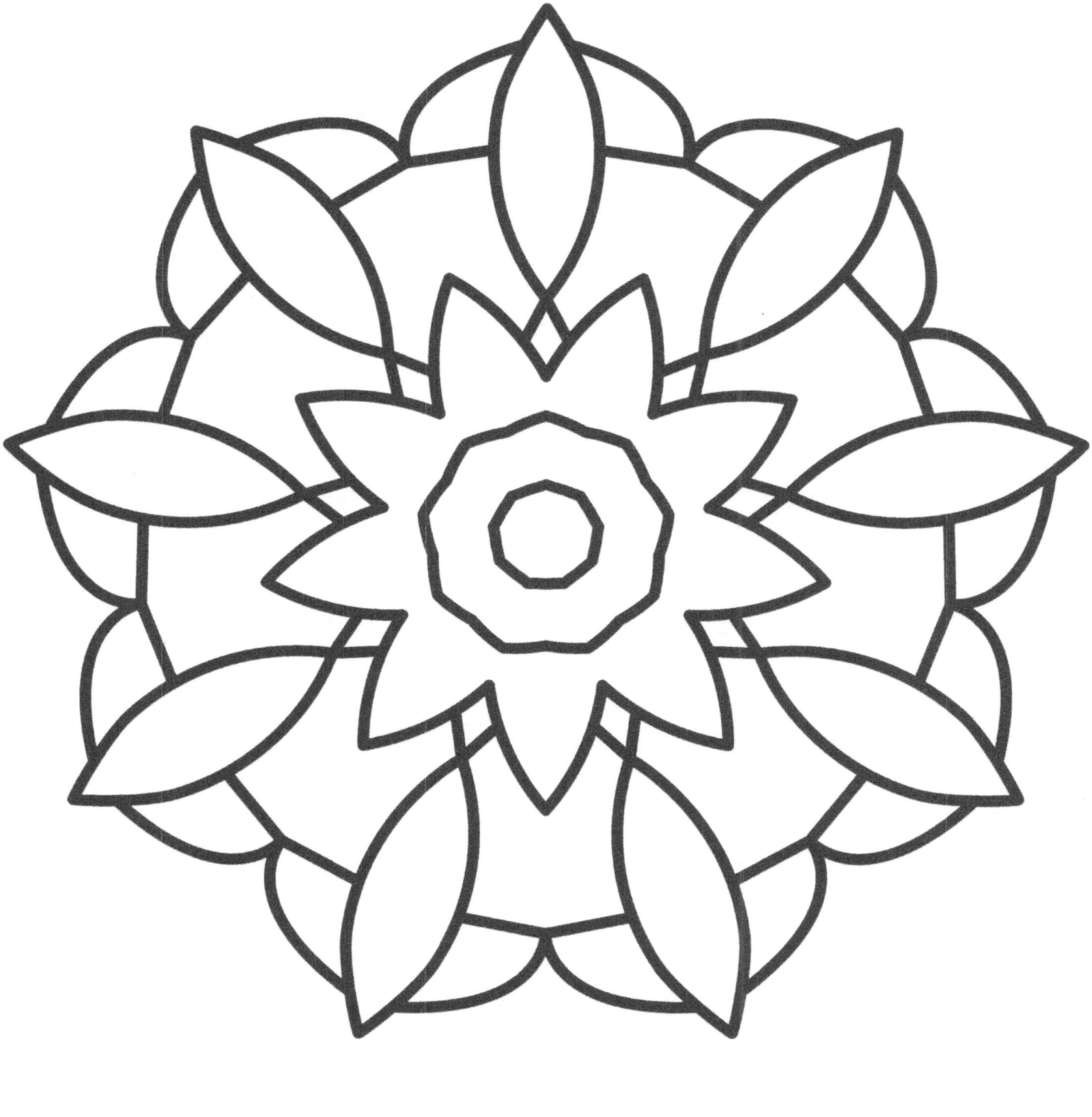

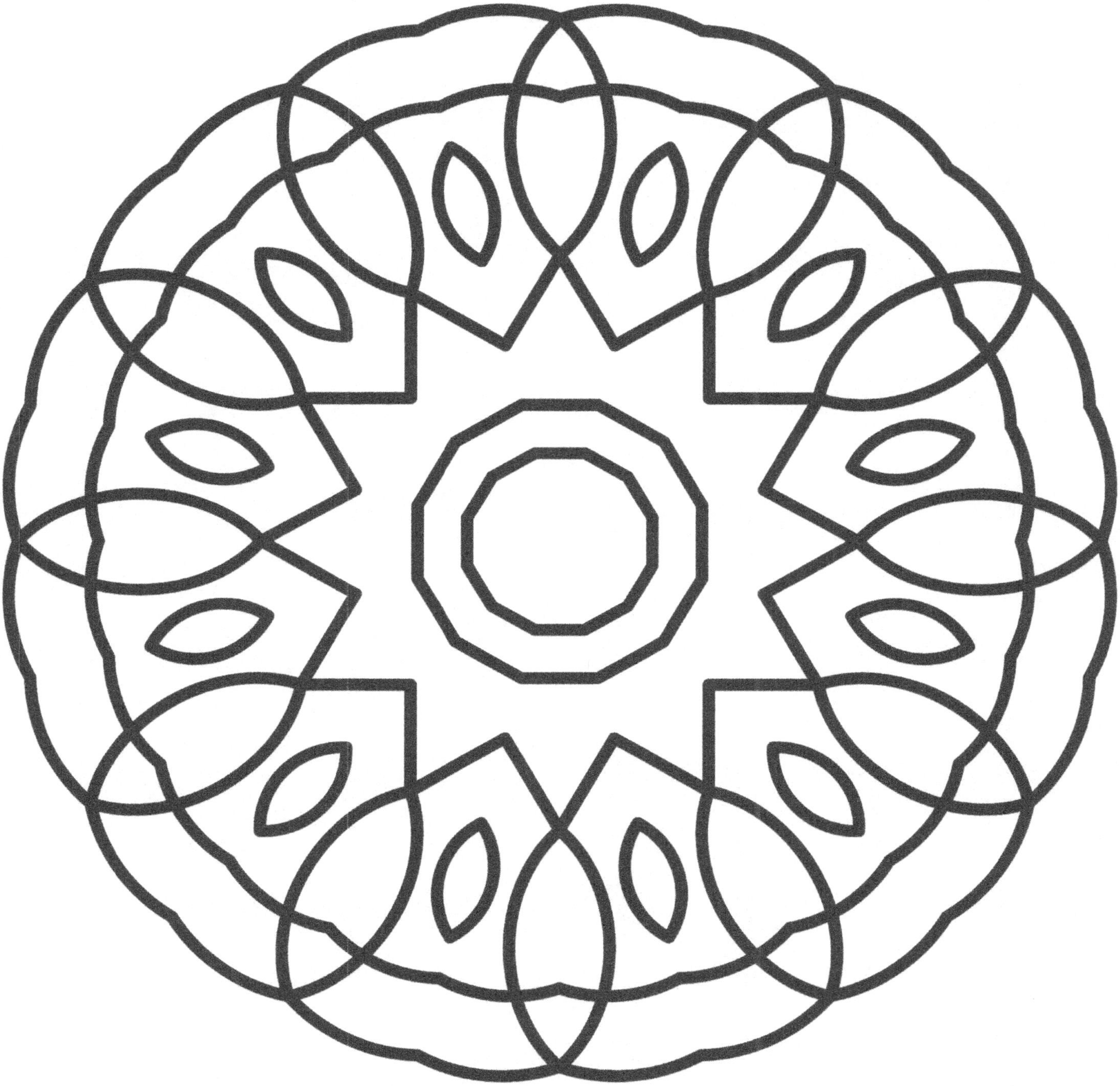

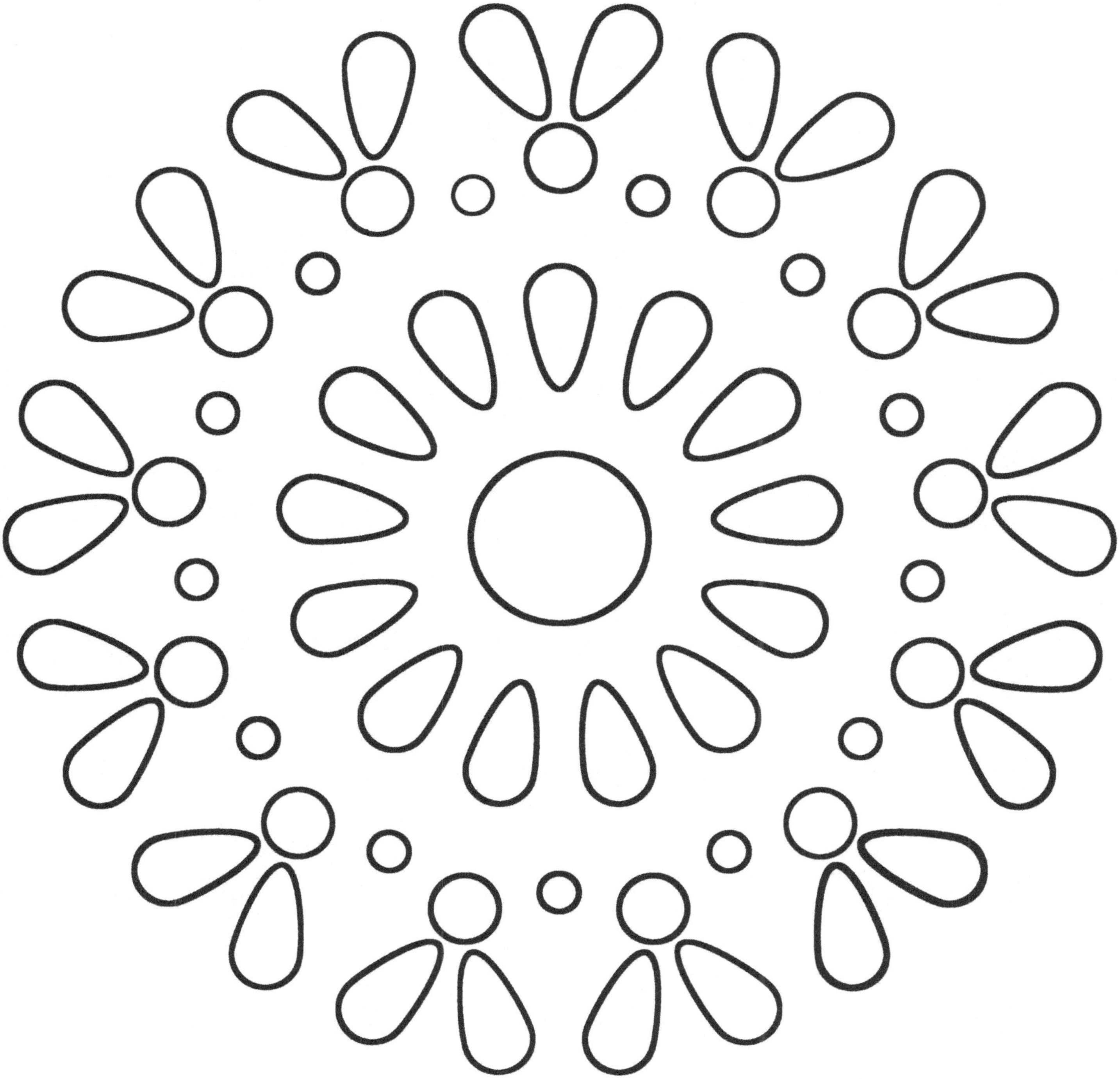

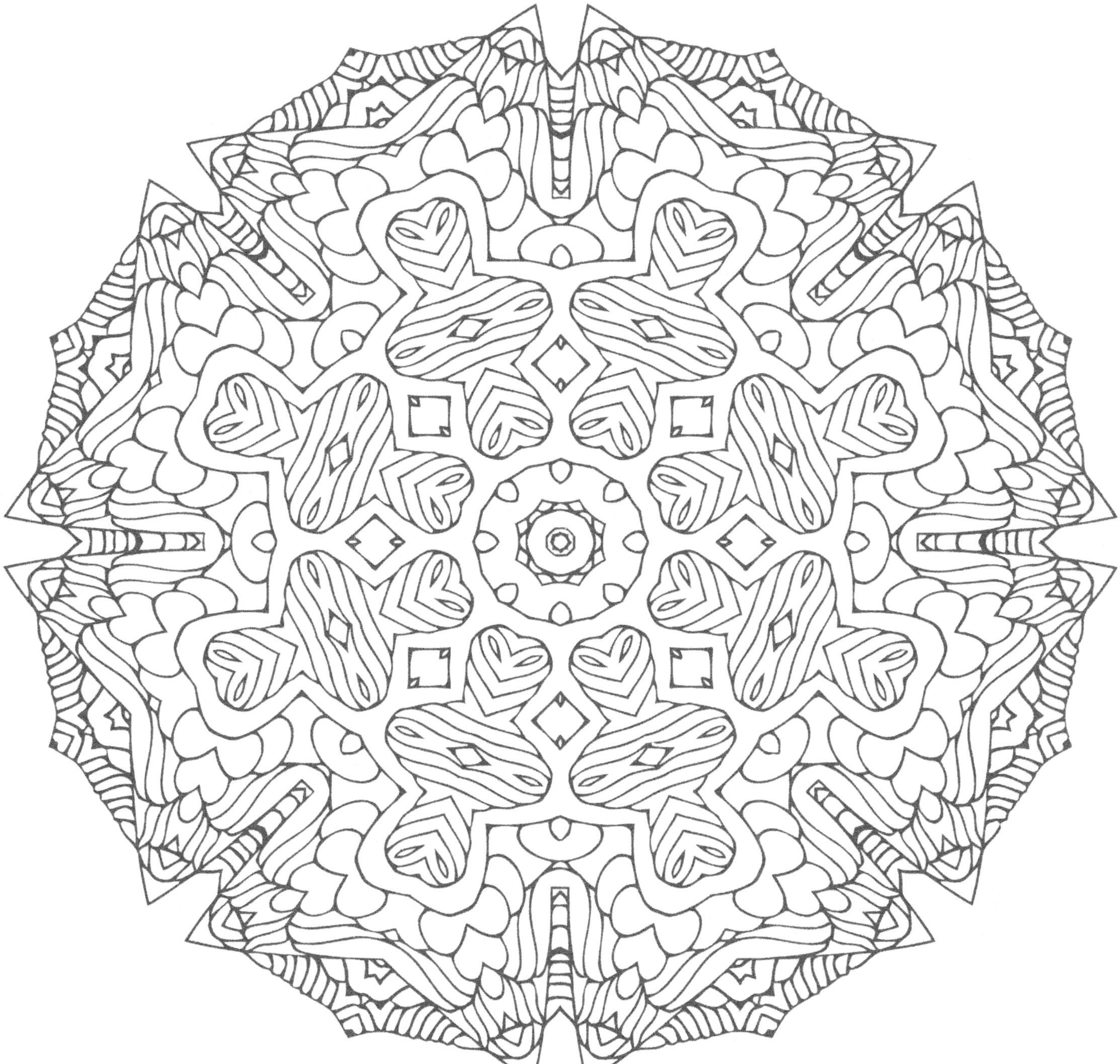

Made in United States
Orlando, FL
14 April 2023

32064669R00059